Everyday Things

An A–Z Guide

Edited and designed by
BOOKMARK ASSOCIATES, INC.

Editorial Director
Sharon Fass Yates

Editor
Joseph Gonzalez

Author
Christina Wilsdon

Designer
Laura Smyth

Copy Editor
Kristina Bohl

Photo Researchers
Artemis Picture Research
Yvonne Silver, Lois Safrani

Indexer
Aaron Murray

Library of Congress Cataloging-in-Publication Data

Wilsdon, Christina.
    Everyday things: an A–Z guide / by Christina Wilsdon.
        p. cm.—(Watts reference)
    Includes bibliographical references and index.
    ISBN 0-531-11792-8 (lib. bdg.)   0-531-15451-3 (pbk.)
    1. Technology—Dictionaries, Juvenile.
    2. Technology—Dictionaires. I. Title. II. Series.

T48.W77 2001
603—dc21   00-068646

1 2 3 4 5 6 7 8 9 10 R 10 09 08 07 06 05 04 03 02 01

Everyday Things

An A–Z Guide

Written by Christina Wilsdon

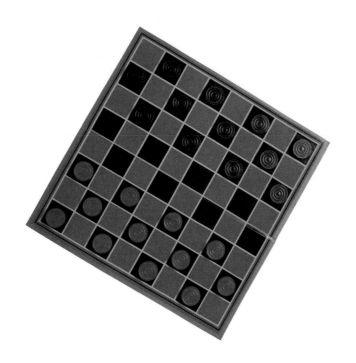

Franklin Watts
A Division of Scholastic Inc.
New York   Toronto   London   Auckland   Sydney
Mexico City   New Delhi   Hong Kong
Danbury, Connecticut

TABLE OF CONTENTS

Alphabet

An alphabet is a system of symbols, or letters, that are used to write words. Each symbol, or letter, stands for a sound.

The alphabet we use is called the Latin, or Roman alphabet. It was developed from other, older alphabets, such as the Greek alphabet. The word *alphabet* comes from the first two letters of the Greek alphabet, *alpha* (α) and *beta* (β).

Cuneiform pressed into a clay tablet.

The Latin alphabet is the world's most widely used alphabet, but half the world uses other systems. People in Russia, for example, use a 32-letter system called the Russian Cyrillic alphabet.

Picture writing

Long before the first alphabet appeared, people communicated with pictures. Prehistoric people painted scenes of animals and humans on the walls of caves. Around 3500 B.C., picture writing was developed by the Sumerian people, who lived in a land that is now part of Iraq. Their writing system is called *cuneiform*, which means "wedge-shaped" and refers to the shape of the marks left by their writing sticks in clay tablets. Each symbol, or pictogram, stood for a different object, such as an ox or a plant.

Around 3000 B.C., the ancient Egyptians developed a system of writing called *hieroglyphics*. This system used not only pictograms but also ideograms, which stood for ideas, and symbols that stood for sounds. A picture of a vulture, for example, could be used to refer to the bird or to the sound "ah."

Hieroglyphic writing was complicated. It involved knowing more than 4,500 pictograms and ideograms, many symbols for sounds, and the many ways to put them together. Only trained scribes, royalty, and priests used hieroglyphics.

The first true alphabet seems to date back to 1800 or 1900 B.C. Its letters were discovered recently, in 1994, carved into soft, limestone cliffs in the desert in the southern part of Egypt. The writers were Semitic people who came into Egypt from the area of Syria and Palestine to work as soldiers or merchants. Archaeologists think this early alphabet is based on Egyptian script. *See also Book; Paper; Pen; Pencil.* ●

From Ox to A

Each of the letters in the Latin alphabet has echoes of its origins. The letter A, for example, started out as a pictogram for "ox." (Turn A upside down and you can still see the ox's head and its two horns.) The wavy letter M began as a pictogram for water.

AMERICAN FLAG

The stars and stripes of the American flag first flew in 1777, less than two years after the beginning of America's revolutionary war against Britain.

The official flag of the English colonies in North America was Britain's flag, the Union Jack. But the colonists began experimenting with different flag designs soon after arriving on North American shores. Early colonists flew a red flag with a white square in the upper left-hand corner.

In 1776, the colonists began flying a flag that was called the Continental Colors or the Grand Union. It had red and white stripes with a small version of the British Union Jack in the upper-left corner. American soldiers flew other rebel flags, including a famous one that showed a coiled rattlesnake ready to strike above the words "Don't Tread on Me."

The stars and stripes

On June 14, 1777, a new version of the Continental Colors became the official flag. It kept the 13 stripes but replaced the small British flag with a star-spangled field of blue. Congress declared that the flag should have 13 stars—one for each of the 13 colonies. Congress did not state how many points the stars should have or how the stars

THEN AND NOW. *The Grand Union flag (left) was first raised in 1776 near George Washington's headquarters outside Boston. Today's flag has 50 stars for the 50 states.*

should be arranged, so some early flags have stars with five or six points arranged in a circle or in rows.

When a new state became part of the United States, a new star and stripe were added to the flag. The flag of 1795, for example, featured 15 stripes and 15 stars. Clearly, the flag was going to become too big or very cluttered over time. So in 1818, lawmakers decided to keep just 13 stripes on the flag to represent the original 13 colonies and to add a new star for each new state. Ever since 1959, when Alaska and Hawaii became states, "Old Glory" has had 50 stars. ●

AMUSEMENT PARK

Amusement parks are places filled with rides and games where children and adults go to have fun. The rides developed long before there were amusement parks.

Merry-go-rounds first whirled 1,600 years ago in Byzantium, an ancient city now known as Istanbul in Turkey. In the late 1600s, French nobles improved their aim by throwing spears at brass rings while riding wooden horses that circled a pole. Servants pushed the merry-go-round to make it spin. This tool became a favorite ride at fairs. Horses and humans continued to pull and push merry-go-rounds until steam power took over in the 1860s.

Roller coaster thrills

Russians rode roller coasters almost 500 years ago. These early versions were steep, ice-covered ramps on which people went sledding. About 200 years ago, French inventors built tracks lined with rollers and sent sleds—and later, cars on wheels—rumbling along them. The first U.S. roller coaster was an old mine train in Pennsylvania that started its new career as a ride about 125 years ago. Mules dragged the cars, loaded with passengers, up a hill. At the top, the

The first U.S. roller coaster was not automated. It was hauled uphill by mules.

mules were loaded on, too, and the cars rolled down the hill at a stately 6 miles per hour.

By the early 1900s, roller coasters were turning riders upside down in loop-the-loops. By 1929, at the peak of coaster-mania, there were about 1,500 coasters nationwide. One of the most famous, the Cyclone, still thrills passengers at Coney Island in New York.

Like the roller coaster, the Ferris wheel is a symbol of amusement parks. Small wheels began turning 600 years ago, but they weren't called Ferris wheels until the arrival of the first steam-powered wheel at the World's Columbian Exposition in Chicago, Illinois, in 1893. The giant wheel, designed by George Ferris, loomed 264 feet (77 meters) high—about the height of a 26-story building. More than one million people paid 50 cents each for a 20-minute ride.

The Exposition looked a lot like a modern amusement park, but such parks really began to grow with the expansion of city trolley-car lines. To attract more passengers, trolley companies built sports fields and amusement parks way out in the country at the end of the lines. Today, more than 300 million people visit amusement parks in the United States every year. ●

BACKPACK

People throughout history have carried loads on their backs in all kinds of strapped-on containers—straw baskets, cloth knapsacks, and leather pouches, for example.

In the early 1900s, backpacks were made of wood and canvas. They often fit

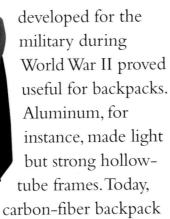

poorly and caused pain. New materials developed for the military during World War II proved useful for backpacks. Aluminum, for instance, made light but strong hollow-tube frames. Today, carbon-fiber backpack frames weigh even less than aluminum ones.

Another improvement for backpacks was synthetics—man-made materials manufactured from chemicals, such as nylon. Synthetics are strong, light, and resistant to water and mildew.

Smaller packs without frames are often called knapsacks or daypacks. This kind of pack is used by students as a book bag. ●

BALLOON

People have been flying in hot-air balloons since 1783, when the Montgolfier brothers of France took to the skies in a basket strapped to a blue and gold paper balloon filled with hot air. Smaller toy balloons have a more ancient history. At least 2,200 years

ago, the Chinese crafted paper balloons that bobbed on the ends of sticks. Native American children played with balloons made from the bladders of animals.

After the first hot-air balloon took off, people began buying toy paper balloons filled with hot air. Soon they switched to balloons made of fabric that could be filled with hydrogen—a gas that is lighter than air but which burns and explodes easily.

Rubber balloons became popular after 1839, when a way to make strong, thin, stretchy rubber was invented. Today, balloons are made from a liquid rubber called latex. To form the balloons, rows of aluminum

shapes are dipped into vats of colored latex. Brushes rub the tops of the mold to make the rolled lip on the balloon's open end. After the latex dries, the balloons are washed and removed from the molds. Then the balloons are packaged for sale. Latex balloons can be blown up with air or with helium. Helium is a lighter-than-air gas, like hydrogen, but it does not explode.

All balloons were round until 1912, when the first sausage-shaped balloons were sold. By the 1950s, people were twisting balloons to make animal shapes, and balloon makers soon began selling long, skinny balloons for this purpose. Silver-foil balloons, which hold helium longer than latex balloons, became popular in the 1970s. ●

BANDAGE

In ages past, injured people pressed cobwebs to their wounds to stop bleeding. Ancient Egyptians wrapped their wounds with linen bandages, usually smeared with healing substances from plants.

The practice of bandaging didn't change for hundreds of years. In the late 1870s, a pharmacist named Robert Johnson came up with the idea of making sterile bandages of cotton and gauze and wrapping them in individual packages. These bandages were germ-free until they were opened in the operating room. He and his brothers formed the Johnson & Johnson Company in 1886 to make and sell the bandages. But these early bandages were not self-sticking. It took another 34 years for the self-sticking bandage to be invented.

Mr. Dickson's idea

Earle Dickson was an employee at Johnson & Johnson, whose wife often cut or burned her fingers while preparing food. Each time, Dickson would have to bandage the wound with cotton gauze and adhesive tape. After a while, he began to wonder if he could make something that could be applied more easily. So Dickson took small bits of gauze and stuck them to a long strip of adhesive tape. Then he covered the strip with a nonsticky material and rolled the whole thing up. Whenever his wife needed a bandage, all she had to do was cut a piece off. And that's how the Band-Aid® was born in 1920.

Since then, self-sticking bandages have improved. Rows of little air holes were added to keep cuts dry and help speed up healing. In 1940, a little red string was added to Band-Aid® wrappers to make them easier to open.

Plastic Band-Aids® came on the scene in 1951 and colorfully decorated ones in 1956.

The butterfly-shaped bandage (left) is used to keep deep cuts tightly closed.

People can now buy self-sticking bandages with pads that have germ-killing ointments. Band-Aids® are so popular that most people use the name for any kind of small, self-sticking bandage. *See also Tape.* ●

BASEBALL

The game of baseball is often called America's national pastime because it is so popular. Its origins, however, lie in old English bat-and-ball games. One of these games is called rounders. It is similar to baseball, but is played on a smaller field. Players run between posts instead of bases, and they hit the ball with a bat that is less than half the size of a baseball bat.

English settlers brought their games with them to the American colonies. As time went by, the colonists played variations of the old games, giving them colorful names, such as "one old cat, two old cat, three old cat," town ball, and the New York Game. These early games could be wild. For example, players were allowed to "tag" a runner out by throwing a ball at him!

In 1845, Alexander Cartwright, the head of an organization called the New York Knickerbocker Base Ball Club, set down rules for the game. Cartwright also designed the baseball diamond, with the batter at home plate, and decided that each team should have nine players. The first game played under Cartwright's rules took place on June 19, 1846, in Hoboken, New Jersey. It lasted only four innings. Nine innings became the official length of a baseball game in 1857.

The game today

Today, the baseball diamond still measures 90 feet (27.4 meters) along each side, as Cartwright laid it out in his original design. The nine players on a baseball team include the pitcher, the catcher (who squats behind home plate), a baseman at each base, a shortstop (who plays in between second and third base), and three outfielders who play in left, center, and right field. There is often a tenth player, called the designated hitter, who bats for the pitcher.

Players use a padded leather glove, called a mitt, when they are on the field. Batters in professional games always swing wooden bats, never aluminum ones. A bat may measure up to 42 inches (106.7 cm) long. The ball weighs about 5 ounces (142 grams). At its center is a small ball made of rubber and cork, which is wrapped in layers of yarn and covered with leather.

Professional baseball teams belong to one of two leagues: the National League or the American League. Every year since 1903, the top teams from each league have played against each other in the World Series. The National Baseball Hall of Fame and Museum, located in Cooperstown, New York, honors baseball's greatest players, umpires, managers, and executives. *See also Basketball; Football; Soccer.* ●

A Little League World Series game in Williamsport, Pennsylvania.

BASKETBALL

The game of basketball was invented in 1891 by James Naismith, a physical education teacher at a college in Springfield, Massachusetts. He wanted an indoor activity his students could play during the long, cold winters. The game was very popular and spread rapidly to other schools.

Naismith's new game had 13 rules based on ideas borrowed from other sports. Then, as now, players scored by getting the ball into the opposing team's basket. The ball could not be carried, but only thrown to other players, or bounced (dribbled) as a player ran with it. In those first games, players used a soccer ball, which they tried to dunk into wooden peach baskets mounted at either end of the gym.

Naismith kept the bottoms in the baskets, so the ball stayed inside when a player scored.

At first, the courts were crowded with up to 18 players. In 1897, the rules changed to limit each team to only five players on the court. Other aspects of basketball also changed over time. Peach baskets were replaced by wire baskets in 1892. Wire baskets were replaced by metal hoops with fiber nets in 1893. The nets were still shut at the bottom and stayed that way until 1912. Backboards appeared in 1895. The rules changed again in the 1930s to make the game faster and more exciting for spectators.

New shots

Until 1936, basketball players stood still and used both hands to toss the ball at the hoop. In that year, a player from California's Stanford University introduced the one-handed shot.

Ten years later, Joe Fulk of the Philadelphia Warriors amazed spectators by jumping high and tossing the ball at the net with one hand. This jump shot is still the most popular shot in basketball today.
See also Baseball; Football; Soccer. ●

BATHTUB

If you lived about 120 years ago, your bathtub may have been nothing more than a large metal basin set in front of the fireplace. You would bathe in water carried into the house in a bucket, then heated over the fire before being poured into the basin. Other family members may have used the bath water before you, and younger siblings would use it after you. Most likely, you had only one bath a week, on Saturday night.

Today, a bathroom with a porcelain or plastic tub—or at least a shower stall—is a standard feature of a modern home. Private tubs, however, were once luxuries enjoyed only by the wealthy. One of the oldest tubs in existence is a clay bathtub found in the royal palace on the Greek island of Crete. It dates back to 1700 B.C. and was used by a queen.

The ups and downs of baths

Although most people in early civilizations didn't have private bathtubs, in some societies, they were able to use public baths. Ancient Rome had huge tiled and heated public baths that held thousands of people. Most people bathed at least once a day.

After Rome fell in 476, the use of public baths declined in much of Europe. In Japan, China, northern Africa, and the Middle East, however, people still enjoyed spectacular bathhouses.

By the 1700s, Europeans were using bathtubs in the privacy of their homes. Some used wooden tubs, which were leaky and smelled sour after long use. By the late 1700s, metal tubs replaced wooden ones.

A modern bathtub holds about 40 gallons of water (38 liters).

Likewise, settlers in North America occasionally bathed in copper tubs or wooden tubs lined with tin. These tubs were filled and emptied by hand, although some had a drain hole. Taking baths, however, was generally frowned upon. As late as 1845, Boston lawmakers made it illegal to take a bath unless ordered to do so by a doctor!

By the 1900s, bathtubs were common in North America. Most had legs that held them above the floor. Floor-level tubs, like those we use today, were introduced in 1911. Tub and shower units appeared a year later. *See also Comb and Hairbrush; Toilet; Toothbrush and Toothpaste.* ●

Battery

A battery is an object that makes electricity when chemical reactions occur inside of it. Batteries come in three basic types: dry cell, wet cell, and button batteries.

A flashlight battery is an example of a dry cell. This type of battery contains a paste that conducts electricity. Inside a wet cell battery is a liquid that conducts electricity. A car battery is a wet cell battery.

Button batteries, which are used in watches and cameras, are very small and powerful. They use lithium metal to conduct electricity.

A battery's power is measured in volts. The term *volt* honors the Italian physicist Alessandro Volta, who built the first battery around 1800. He stacked up pairs of zinc and copper disks, with disks of cardboard soaked in saltwater between each pair. The chemical reaction between the metals and salt created an electrical current. ●

Bed

"Good night, sleep tight, don't let the bedbugs bite." This childhood rhyme represented a real problem for prehistoric humans, who slept on piles of fur and leaves on the ground. Such beds attracted bugs and mice, too. To avoid these pests, early humans eventually began building above-the-ground beds made of slim logs and woven fibers that were supported by forked tree branches.

Ancient Egyptians slept on woven beds covered with linen sheets. Bed canopies and curtains were used to keep out mosquitoes. In other ancient cultures, beds were used for dining (so diners could recline during meals) as well as sleeping. The ancient Greeks used bronze, wooden, or wicker beds with soft pillows filled with feathers and wool. The ancient Romans stuffed cloth bags with wool, straw, or feathers to make mattresses.

From the late 1400s, luxurious beds became very popular among the nobility in western Europe. Wealthy people lavished money on expensive sheets and blankets. Four-poster beds, with canopies on top and curtains all around, also became fashionable.

But most people still slept on mattresses that were straw-filled and uncomfortable. The invention of the coiled metal spring in the early 1800s improved the comfort of

A modern mattress with inner-springs is made cozy with lots of pillows and colorful blankets.

sleepers forever. These springs were first used in carriage seats but were adapted into cone shapes by an American, James Liddy, in the 1850s. Liddy's springs were used to make the first bouncy inner-spring mattresses.

Inner-spring mattresses remained luxury items into the 1920s. Most people still slept on stuffed mattresses. They made the switch when inner springs became affordable.

In the 1960s, plastic mattresses filled with water or air became popular. Today, some people choose to sleep on Japanese-style *futons,* mattresses stuffed with cotton and other fabrics. ●

BICYCLE

The first bicycle was the *draisienne,* a machine that did not have pedals. It was built in 1817 by a German engineer, Baron Karl von Drais. The rider sat on the bike's seat with his or her feet on the ground and ran, occasionally picking up the feet in order to coast.

In 1861, a French coach maker, Pierre Michaux, built a bicycle that had a very large front wheel and a small rear wheel. It was called a velocipede. The wheels were made of metal, and the large front one had pedals attached to it. Soon, manufacturers were making velocipedes with ever-larger front wheels because a large wheel carried a rider farther with each pedaling motion than a

smaller one. By 1868, velocipedes featured a rear-wheel brake. It slowed the bike a little, but riders were still advised to crash into bushes if the bike went out of control!

In 1885, velocipedes were replaced by the Rover safety bicycle. Its wheels were the

THEN AND NOW. *The old velocipede (left) was also called a "boneshaker" because riders were shaken up by bumps and pebbles on rutted roads. Today's bikes (above) offer smoother, more comfortable, and safer rides.*

same size, and it was powered by pedals attached to a chain linked to the rear wheel, as on modern bikes. The ride was still rough, but safer than on a velocipede.

In 1888, air-filled tires appeared on bicycles for the first time after a Scottish inventor, John Dunlop, turned a rubber garden hose into tires for his son's tricycle. By 1906, bike gears were introduced that allowed riders to climb hills more easily.

Bikes today come in a variety of styles. Racing and touring bikes are designed for speed. Mountain bikes can be ridden on steep, rough roads. *See also Wheel.* ●

BOARD GAME

A board game is any game that involves moving pieces from place to place on a board that has a unique route, scene, or other design on it.

People have been playing board games for at least 9,000 years! Archaeologists digging in Syria and Israel have discovered boards with rows of holes that date back to 7000 B.C. They have also found boards, small black-and-white playing pieces, and an early form of dice in tombs in Mesopotamia, an ancient land that is now part of Iraq.

Inside Egyptian tombs, scientists have discovered sets of the board game Senet that date as far back as 2700 B.C. Senet was very popular in ancient Egypt, as carvings of people huddled around the game reveal. Like other board games, it involved moving pieces from a starting point to a finishing point. The trip across the Senet board represented a trip from the moment of death to the arrival in the ancient Egyptian world of the afterlife. A version of Senet reached Europe and later became the game we call backgammon.

Games from far and wide

Other popular games have been around for ages, too. The ancient Chinese began playing Go around 2000 B.C. Chess originated in India 1,500 years ago. Another Indian game is Parcheesi®, which dates back to the year 600. Indian children played *Gyan chaupar,* the distant ancestor of Chutes and Ladders®,

first played by American children in the 1950s and still popular today.

Clue®, Sorry®, Scrabble®, Candy Land,® and many other board games created since 1950 are also still going strong today. Candy Land®, produced by the Milton Bradley Company, remains the first board game played by most American children.

Over 100 million copies of Monopoly® have been sold since 1935. It has been played on a ceiling, underwater, and in a moving elevator for 16 days!

One of the most popular board games in modern times is Monopoly®. Players buy, sell, and rent properties, making or losing money as they move around the board. Monopoly® was created in 1933 by Charles Darrow of Pennsylvania to amuse himself while he was out of work. He named the properties after streets in Atlantic City, New Jersey. When he tried to sell the idea, the Parker Brothers company said the game was too difficult. Two years later, they changed their minds and purchased the rights to Darrow's game. *See also Checkers; Chess.* ●

Book

The first "books" were very heavy sets of clay tablets kept in a box. They were made about 5,000 years ago in Mesopotamia, which is where Iraq is now.

Books became much lighter after the ancient Egyptians started making thick sheets to write on from the stems of papyrus plants. Papyrus sheets were rolled around a spool and unrolled for reading. These books were stored in the first libraries.

Books written on parchment sheets were also rolled up. Parchment is very thin leather that has been treated to make it soft and smooth for writing. Parchment sheets could also be bound together to make left-hand and right-hand pages, like pages in a modern book. This made reading easier.

Books for everybody

Parchment was used in Europe until paper, a Chinese invention, became available in the Middle Ages. However, each book was handmade, hand-lettered, and hand-illustrated. Books were usually made only for nobles, priests, and scholars—not ordinary people.

A new age dawned around 1450 when Johann Gutenberg, a German goldsmith, invented a printing press with moveable letters. Gutenberg discovered a way to shape letters quickly and inexpensively from a mixture of metals. Workers poured the mix into molds to make the letters. One good worker could make up to 4,000 letters a day. Gutenberg also created a black ink to spread on the letters and the machine that pressed the ink onto paper.

Thanks to the printing press, books could be made cheaply and quickly. Over the next 500 years, books became more common. In the 1800s, automated printing presses were introduced. By the end of the 1900s, computers sped up the printing process, and e-books were invented. These are computer-like, hand-held devices that have screens for reading.
See also Library; Paper. ●

Printing in China

The Chinese began printing in the 600s. Printers etched Chinese characters (word symbols) onto wood. Then they rolled ink onto the wood and pressed paper to its surface to print a page. Because there are thousands of Chinese characters, Chinese printers did not develop moveable type (characters that could be moved and re-used). That was what Gutenberg did.

Bowling

Bowling is a game in which a player rolls a ball down a 60-foot (18-meter) lane at a set of ten pins arranged in a triangle. The ball, made of plastic or a special type of hard rubber, has three finger holes in it to help the player hold it. It may weigh up to 16 pounds (7.3 kg). The pins are made of maple wood encased in plastic.

The lane, made of wood or plastic, is highly polished and waxed. Gutters on either side of the lane catch balls that roll off it. Special bowling shoes help players slide their feet properly on the floor.

A machine returns the balls to the head of the lane. Another machine, called the automatic pinsetter, sweeps away any pins that are knocked down. It also sets up new pins for each new round, or frame, of bowling. This job used to be done by workers called pinboys before the invention of the pinsetter in 1952.

Nine pins

People bowled long before there were plastic balls and pinsetters, however. A ball and a set of nine pins were discovered in the grave of an Egyptian child that dates back to 3200 B.C. Nine-pin bowling became the standard in Europe by the 1500s.

European settlers brought the game with them to the New World. In 1841, Connecticut made it illegal to play nine-pin bowling because it encouraged people to gamble. Legend says a devoted fan of the game got around the law by using ten pins instead of nine. Americans have played ten-pin bowling ever since. ●

Braces

Braces are devices that straighten crooked teeth and correct what is called a "bad bite." A bad bite occurs when the upper and lower teeth don't line up properly with each other.

Braces are made of metal or plastic bands and wire. Rubber bands attached to the braces slowly and steadily pull teeth back or straighten them out. Braces are fitted by orthodontists—dentists who specialize in straightening teeth.

Having straight teeth not only improves your smile, but also prevents jaw and dental problems. Crooked teeth, for example, are difficult to keep clean, so straightening them helps prevent tooth decay and gum disease.

Braces used to be made of heavy, thick metal bands and wires. Modern ones are made of thin metal bands or clear plastic and ceramic patches that are glued to the teeth. Colorful rubber bands and thin, flexible wire hold everything together and exert steady pressure on teeth. *See also Toothbrush and Toothpaste.* ●

BREAD

Bread was the first food ever made by humans. Archaeologists have found the remains of prehistoric breads made from wild wheat and weed seeds mixed with water. These early breads were flat, like a tortilla, and hard because they did not contain leavening agents—ingredients that would make the breads puff up while they were being made.

Look closely at a slice of bread, and you'll see that it is dotted with holes. These holes were made by a leavening agent. A fungus called yeast is the most common leavening agent in bread. When yeast is added to bread dough, it reacts with sugars in the ingredients and gives off an invisible gas called carbon dioxide, as well as alcohol. The bubbles puff up the dough and leave behind the holes that you see in a slice of bread.

Making a loaf of bread requires little more than flour, yeast, salt, and water—and kneading. Kneading is a way of mixing

bread dough by squeezing it. The ancient Egyptians kneaded bread with their feet. Today, people who bake at home knead dough by hand, pushing and pressing it on a flat surface. They may also put it into a bread machine, which kneads the bread with a paddle. Commercial bakeries process dough in large mixers equipped with special dough hooks that do the kneading. *See also Cereal; Sandwich.* ●

Light Bread

The ancient Egyptians may have discovered leavened bread by accident. A baker may have left a batch of flour and water out in the open, and some yeast spores in the air settled on it. When the dough was ready to be baked, it had puffed up in size.

Butter

Butter is a mixture of fat, water, and salt. It is made from cream—a pale yellow, fatty substance found in milk. Whipping the cream makes it solid and turns it into butter. This process is called churning.

The first people to churn butter may have been nomads who roamed Central Asia with herds of animals. In ancient times, these nomads packed their food in leather bags and strapped them to the backs of horses and camels. Milk carried in such bags turned into butter as it sloshed around.

The ancient Celtic people of Europe ate butter, too. They kept it fresh by adding lots of salt to it. The ancient Greeks and Romans preferred to spread butter in their hair to style it.

Churning

Up until about 150 years ago, people churned butter by hand. The cream was poured into a tall wooden or clay container called a butter churn. A paddle called a dasher sat inside. Its handle poked out of the top. The person making butter plunged the dasher up and down in the cream until it thickened. This task was usually the responsibility of women and children.

Churning turned the cream into bits of butter floating in a liquid called buttermilk. The buttermilk was poured off and saved for other uses. Then the butter was rinsed in cold water. Finally, it was packed into butter molds to shape it.

The first butter factory started in 1856. Today, about one-third of the world's cow's milk is used for butter. Stores sell salted and unsalted butter, which is also called "sweet" butter," but no sugar is added to it. Whipped butter is mixed with air to make it spread more easily.

In India, butter is made from the milk of water buffaloes. In Tibet, it is made from yak milk. Some people in the Middle East use camel-milk butter—just like the nomads who "invented" the creamy spread. *See also Milk.* ●

Button

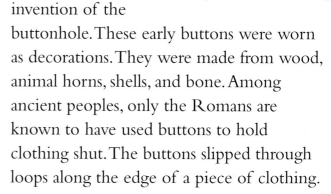

Buttons appeared on people's clothing over 4,300 years before the invention of the buttonhole. These early buttons were worn as decorations. They were made from wood, animal horns, shells, and bone. Among ancient peoples, only the Romans are known to have used buttons to hold clothing shut. The buttons slipped through loops along the edge of a piece of clothing.

Buttons began to be used as fasteners in the 1200s, but they continued to be valued as decorations. Because buttons were made by hand, they were expensive. Wealthy people's clothes had buttons made of glass, ivory, gold, and jewels. King Frances I of

France, who lived from 1494–1547, adored buttons. One of his formal garments sparkled with 13,600 gold buttons!

Buttons became more affordable and widely available in the 1700s when they began to be machine-made. In the United States, metal workers made buttons of brass, silver, and, starting in 1802, copper.

Buttons on clothing today are usually made of plastic, metal, mother-of-pearl, or "vegetable ivory," which comes from a nut. ●

CALCULATOR

A calculator is a device that does math quickly. It can only process numbers. It can't process letters or other symbols as a computer does.

The first calculator was probably the human hand. Counting on fingers and using fingers to stand for numbers helped early people calculate swiftly. Ancient Romans added or subtracted by moving pebbles that represented numbers. The word *calculator* actually comes from the Latin word *calculi,* which means "pebbles."

The first mechanical calculator could only add and subtract. It was invented in 1642 by Blaise Pascal, a 19-year-old Frenchman. A German mathematician, Gottfried Wilhelm von Leibniz, figured out in 1671 how to make the calculator multiply and divide, too.

How a calculator works

When you press a number on a calculator's keyboard, it sends an electrical signal to a component called the microprocessor. It's the microprocessor that figures out the answer to your math problem. The answer is then sent as an electrical signal to your calculator's small screen.

How your answer appears depends on whether your calculator has an LCD or an LED screen. LCD stands for Liquid Crystal Display. An LCD screen has a substance called liquid crystal floating behind it.

Normally, the liquid crystal reflects light like a mirror. When electricity flows through certain patterns etched in the back of the screen, however, it causes the liquid crystal in those areas to stop reflecting light. These dark areas form the numbers we see. Many clocks and watches use LCDs, too.

LED stands for Light Emitting Diodes, which are arrangements of crystals that turn electricity into light. LEDs glow when activated.

While an LCD screen glows softly and features dark numbers, an LED screen is dark with bright numbers on it. *See also Computer; Numbers.* ●

CALENDAR

A calendar is a system for dividing a year into days, weeks, and months. The first calendars may have been made by Stone Age people who carved neat lines into animal bones 30,000 years ago. The lines seem to record the time it takes the moon to change its shape through a full cycle of phases.

A crescent moon is the first sliver we see of the moon's changing shape. As days pass, we see more and more of the moon that is lit by the sun. The sliver becomes a half-moon (called a first-quarter moon), and then a full moon. Afterwards, we see less and less of the moon until we can't see it at all. Then a new sliver appears, and the cycle starts again. The moon's cycle takes about one month to occur, and our calendar month is based on it.

Crescent moon   *First-quarter moon*   *Full moon*

The moon, however, does not orbit the Earth exactly 12 times a year. It completes 12 cycles in a little more than 354 days, or 11 days short of a full year. As a result, early moon-based calendars did not stay in sync with actual seasons and the passage of time. People have tinkered with the calendar for thousands of years to cope with this mismatch—adding days here, subtracting days there. In 46 B.C., the Roman ruler Julius Caesar added an extra day to every fourth year, making it a "leap year."

The calendar used in many parts of the world today is called the Gregorian calendar. It is named for Pope Gregory XIII, who made important changes to the calendar in 1582.

Naming months

The names of the months hark back to Roman times. January and March are named after the Roman gods Janus and Mars, and May comes from the goddess Maia. February is named for a Roman festival. April's name comes from a Latin word meaning "open," perhaps because so many flowers open up in April. June may be named for the Roman goddess Juno or for a word meaning "youth." July honors Julius Caesar, and August is named for the Roman emperor Augustus.

September, October, November, and December mean—in order—seventh, eighth, ninth, and tenth month. Today, these months are really the ninth through twelfth months. Their names date back to early Roman calendars in which the year began on March 1 instead of January 1. ●

	S	M	T	W	T	F	S
JUNE					1	2	3
	4	5	6	7	8	9	10
	11	12	13	14	15	16	17
	18	19	20	21	22	23	24
	25	26	27	28	29	30	

CAMERA

A camera works by allowing light to shine through a lens into a darkened chamber. There the light strikes film. The film is covered with chemicals that react to light. The scene in front of the camera is recorded on the film as an upside-down image. Then the film is treated with chemicals and the image is enlarged to form pictures that are printed on paper. The treatment process is called developing.

Dark rooms

The idea of the camera dates back centuries. In ancient Greece and Arabia, it was known that light shining through a very small hole could produce an upside-down image. People used this technique for entertainment. They poked a tiny hole in a wall of a darkened room and then viewed images of what was going on outside. This room came to be known as the *camera obscura*, which is Latin for "dark room."

The *camera obscura* got smaller over time. In the 1600s, it went from being a room to a small box with lenses and mirrors. The image produced by the box fell on a piece of paper, where an artist could trace it.

Discoveries about chemicals that are sensitive to light led to the invention of film. A French chemist, Joseph-Nicéphore

Niepce, made the first photographs in 1827. He used metal plates coated with light-sensitive chemicals. Another Frenchman, Louis Daguerre, found a faster way to take pictures. His pictures, called daguerrotypes, became very popular. William Henry Fox Talbot, an Englishman, experimented with light-sensitive paper. He used dark images to make light ones and vice versa—just as we make photographic prints from negatives today. He called his images calotypes.

Kodaks and digitals

Daguerrotypes and calotypes were replaced in the 1850s by pictures taken on glass plates. Prints of the pictures were then made from the plates.

Modern cameras adjust focus and speed automatically. Some even track your eye movements to focus where you are looking!

In 1884, George Eastman, an American, invented a way of putting film on a roll of paper. Eastman also designed the first easy-to-use box camera in 1888. He called it the Kodak. A year later, Eastman invented plastic film that could be easily loaded into the camera and removed by the user.

Color film first became available in 1942. Polaroids, which develop pictures on the spot, came onto the market in 1947.

Today, there are cameras that don't use film at all. Digital cameras store images in the form of electronic signals. This information can be downloaded onto a computer, seen on a screen, printed out on paper, or sent to friends by e-mail. *See also Movie.* ●

CAN

Preserving foods in cans or jars is called *canning*. Canning involves heating food to a very high temperature to kill all the bacteria and other germs that make food go bad. The can is then quickly sealed.

A French chef and candy maker, Nicolas Appert, invented canning in 1809. He won a national contest to find a way to preserve food for use by France's army. Appert sealed food in glass bottles and jars and then boiled them.

Canned foods

By 1810, English canning factories began preserving food in tin cans. The food was put in and a tiny hole was left in the lid while the food was heated. Afterward, the hole was quickly sealed. Then the cans were heated again.

Foods preserved in cans became widely available by the mid-1800s. In the United States, Civil War soldiers consumed many different kinds of canned foods, including condensed milk packaged by a woman named Gail Borden. The Borden Company still sells canned milk today.

In 1958, a new kind of can for food came on the market: the aluminum can. You know it as the kind of can that soda pop comes in. Aluminum cans are lighter in weight than tin ones and cost less to make. Cans with a thinner tin coating soon followed.

Today, the United States makes over 60 billion tin cans and nearly 100 billion aluminum cans for both food and nonfood products. It's a good thing we recycle cans! Aluminum cans can be processed into new ones in just eight weeks.

Pop-tops

Cans with pop-tops were introduced in 1963. A pop-top is a ring attached to a small, teardrop-shaped piece of metal that is pulled off to reveal a drinking hole. Pop-top tabs, however, became a huge litter problem because so many people tossed the tabs aside after opening the can. This problem led to the invention of the modern pop-top, which stays attached to the can. *See also Frozen Food; Refrigerator.* ●

Tins and Cans

The first tin cans were made of metal coated with tin. In England, they were called "tin canisters," but people there soon shortened this term to "tins." Americans shortened the phrase to "cans." Today's tin cans are made of steel coated with a thin layer of tin. Some are coated inside with enamel to prevent certain kinds of food from reacting with the metal.

CANDY

Liking sweet things probably helped our prehistoric ancestors survive. If a fruit tasted sweet, it usually meant that it was ripe and safe to eat—instead of being unripe or perhaps poisonous. Today, sweet foods still appeal to our taste buds.

The ancient Egyptians first made candy about 4,000 years ago by mixing honey with herbs, nuts, spices, seeds, figs, and dates as well as colorful dyes. The ancient Greeks and Romans ate almonds dipped in honey.

In Persia, an ancient land now called Iran, farmers grew sugar cane, which could be chewed to bring out its sweetness or crushed and boiled to make a thick, dark-brown sugar. Over hundreds of years, the cultivation of sugar cane spread to other countries.

Sugary treats

In the 1200s, some sugar from sugar cane began to be used to make candy. Most European candy, however, was made by pharmacists. These candies contained herbs to cure stomachaches, ease coughs, and soothe sore throats.

In the 1300s, candy makers in Venice, Italy, spun sugar into large yet delicate sculptures. Sugar was also mixed with ground almonds to create a sweet treat called marzipan, which is still a treat today.

Even though sugar-cane cultivation came to the Americas shortly after Columbus first arrived in 1492, candy did not become an everyday treat for a long time. Early English settlers enjoyed other types of sweets, such as as jam and maple syrup. They also made "rock candy" by boiling sugar water, and then letting the sugar form large, clumped crystals.

Candy making really took off after the introduction of candy-making machinery in the late 1800s. Stick candies became popular, though people still made taffy at home. Taffy—a mixture of sugar, molasses, and water boiled together—is tugged and pulled to make it light and fluffy. Taffy-making gatherings were called taffy pulls.

Making candy

Candy is basically a mixture of sugar and water with added colorings, flavors, and other ingredients. Making candy involves boiling sugar water to make a thick syrup. Cooking the syrup at a high temperature makes hard candies, such as lollipops. Cooking the syrup at a low temperature makes soft candies, such as fudge.

Today, Americans eat about 22 pounds of candy per person a year! What's the best-selling candy in the world? Life Savers®. *See also Chocolate; Cookie; Ice Cream; Popcorn.* ●

CAR

The very first car puttered along at about 2 miles (3 km) per hour. It had three wheels and was powered by steam from hot water. Nicolas Cugnot, a French inventor, built it in 1769. The car could not travel farther than one mile.

The first car to run on gasoline, the way modern cars do, was invented about 100 years later, in 1860, by a Belgian living in France named Jean-Joseph Etienne Lenoir. This car was powered by an engine that burned fuel inside of it—an internal combustion engine. It took three hours for Lenoir to drive 6 miles (9.5 km) in his car.

Three-wheeled cars

Many inventors, engineers, and others tinkered with engines and carriages over the next few decades. One of the first successful car manufacturers was a German engineer named Karl Benz. The three-wheeled car that Benz designed was much more powerful than Lenoir's car. Benz began selling his car in 1887.

In 1891, a French engineer named Emile Levassor designed a car with four wheels and an engine up front. Most cars have kept this shape ever since.

Ford's Model T

The early days of automobile history are filled with names that are still familiar to us today—

Chevrolet, Chrysler, and Ford. In 1908, Henry Ford reorganized the Ford Motor Company and sold a car called the Model T for $850. Eighteen years later, a new one cost only $290! Its low price made it possible for millions of people to own a car.

Assembly line

Ford's cars were so inexpensive because he developed a new way of building them in 1913: on an assembly line. Parts of a car rolled along on a moving platform, called a conveyor belt, and were put together by workers standing alongside it. A car could now be built in just 90 minutes instead of three months. This meant a shiny, brand-new Model T rolled out of the factory every 90 seconds! Cars are still built on assembly lines today.

The family car helps keep America on the move. Its basic shape— four wheels and a motor up front—has not changed in more than a century.

Fuel of the future

Most cars use gasoline for fuel, but some use diesel oil. Others run on electric batteries. Automakers are developing new fuels that will be safer for our environment. They are also working with fuel cells, which power the space shuttle, and may one day replace the car's internal combustion engine. *See also Wheel.* ●

Naming the Car

At first, cars were called horseless carriages, because that is what they were: carriages without horses. Later on, names such as oleo locomotive, motor fly, and electrobat were suggested. Finally, the word *automobile* was chosen. It means "self-moving." The word *car* dates back to the 14th century and was used to describe any wheeled vehicle.

Cereal

A cereal is an edible seed, known as grain, that belongs to the family of plants called grasses. Wheat, corn, oats, rice, rye, and barley are all cereals. The food gets its name from Ceres, the Roman goddess of grain. She was honored by festivals called *cerealia*. Today, the word cereal usually means a breakfast food in a colorful box that is poured into a bowl along with milk. Ready-to-eat cereals date back about 150 years and changed the breakfast menu forever.

Fast-food breakfasts

Quick-cooking breakfast oats appeared around 1850. An American named Ferdinand Schumacher thought that people would eat more hot oatmeal if they could cook it quickly. His product inspired another American, Tom Avidon, to grind wheat into a quick-cooking cereal. He called it Cream of Wheat®.

Cold breakfast cereal didn't hit store shelves until 1892, when an American named Henry Perky processed wheat into little biscuits and called it Ceres. Later, the product became known as Shredded Wheat®.

Other cold breakfast cereals soon joined it. Dr. James Jackson developed a bran cereal called Granula. Another doctor, John Harvey Kellogg, and his brother, invented Corn Flakes® in the early 1900s. Dr. Kellogg set up a cereal-making company in Battle Creek, Michigan, where he also ran a health center. One of his patients was a man named Charles W. Post. He started up a rival cereal company featuring a wheat product called Grape-Nuts®. You can still buy these cereals and many new ones, too. ●

CHECKERS

The game of checkers is played by two people on a checkered board that is divided into eight rows. Each row has four light squares and four dark ones that alternate with each other. The squares are often red and black. The playing pieces, called men, move forward on the board's dark squares.

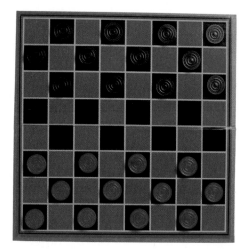

To win the game, you must capture your opponent's pieces. You capture a piece by jumping over it. This allows you to remove it from the board. If your men reach the farthest row on the opposite side of the board, they become kings. Kings can move backward and forward.

No one knows for sure how checkers got started. Games similar to checkers were played under different names and in different countries, beginning with the ancient Egyptians. The ancient Romans played a game called *calculi* that may have been an early form of checkers.

Some experts believe checkers began in France in the 1100s. Others place its origin in England, where the game has long been called *draughts. See also Board Game; Chess.* ●

CHESS

Like checkers, chess is played by two people. Each has 16 chessmen. Eight are called pawns; the other eight are a king, a queen, two bishops, two knights, and two castle towers (rooks). The object of the game is to capture your opponent's king.

Chess is believed to have its origins in India. Around A.D. 500, people in India played a game called *chaturanga,* which means "army." The game traveled to Persia (now called Iran), then to Arabia and Europe.

The word *chess* comes from *shah,* a Persian word for "king." Europeans used the word for all the pieces, not just the king. They changed the Persian pieces, which included elephants, to familiar European characters, such as knights and bishops. Other forms of chess are played in Asia and the Middle East.

Computers were first programmed to play chess in 1957. In 1997, world chess champion Gary Kasparov lost to a computer called Deep Blue. *See also Board Game; Checkers.* ●

CHOCOLATE

Yummy, sweet chocolate comes from the bitter beans of the cacao tree. Processing cacao beans involves letting them ferment and dry, then roasting them and removing their shells. When the roasted beans are ground up, they release a thick liquid called chocolate liquor and a fat called cocoa butter.

Pure and bitter

Pure chocolate is very bitter, as anyone who has nibbled on a square of unsweetened baking chocolate knows! Sweet chocolate contains sugar.

The first people to taste chocolate were the Aztec, Toltec, and Mayan peoples of ancient Mexico. Cacao trees grew naturally in their warm climate and were cultivated there for over 2,500 years. The native peoples brewed the beans from the cacao trees with cornmeal, vanilla, and spices to make a frothy, spicy, bitter drink for royalty. They called this special drink *xocoatl*, which sounded like the word *chocolatl*. It meant "foam water" or "bitter water."

Spanish explorers brought cacao beans back to Europe in the early 1500s. They mixed chocolate with vanilla and sugar to make cocoa. The Spanish were able to keep chocolate a secret for 100 years before the rest of Europe found out about it!

Until the early 1800s, chocolate was used only to make drinks or baked goods. But cocoa butter was a problem in chocolate drinks, because it rose to the top of the liquid and floated there. The drinker had to scoop it out to get rid of it.

Different types of chocolate chips: milk chocolate, white chocolate, and dark chocolate.

Sweet cocoa

Then, in 1828, a Dutch chemist found a way to improve cocoa. He invented a machine that pressed cocoa butter out of chocolate, leaving behind cocoa powder. In the 1840s, an English candy-making firm found that mixing cocoa butter with chocolate liquor made solid chocolate that could be molded into bars and shapes, stayed solid at room temperature, but melted smoothly in the mouth. Some years later, Swiss chocolate makers mixed together milk and chocolate to make delicious milk chocolate.

Today, Americans consume about 11 pounds (5 kg) of chocolate per person a year. The Swiss eat about twice this amount. They would agree with the scientists who named the cacao tree *Theobroma cacao*, which means "cacao, the food of the gods." *See also Candy.*●

Cacao pods growing on a cacao tree.

CLOCKS AND WATCHES

Hours. Minutes. Seconds. We use clocks and watches to measure these chunks of time. In the ancient world, shadows, fire, water, and sand marked the passage of time.

About 3,500 years ago, the Egyptians designed a clock called a sundial. The sundial used the changing length of the sun's shadow on a dial as a way to tell the time of day.

A sundial, however, is useless at night or on a cloudy day. Under these conditions, a burning candle marked with notches kept track of time. The ancient Chinese set fire to knotted ropes, marking time by how long it took the flame to burn its way from knot to knot.

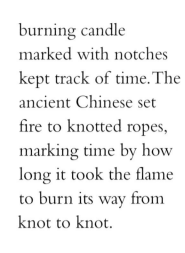

Cuckoo clocks are run by dropping weights—a technology invented 1,000 years ago.

Drip by drip

The ancient Chinese and Egyptians used water clocks, too, as did the Greeks and Romans. The water clock was a bucket with a hole in it. Water dripped out of the hole. Marks on the bucket were compared with the level of water left inside to measure how much time had passed. Some Greek water clocks were very complex. They could ring bells, blow whistles, and turn dials. But water clocks were not exact and they froze in winter.

Neither weather nor darkness, however, can affect a sand clock, also called an hourglass. In an hourglass, sand flows down at an even pace from a top globe into a bottom globe. But sand clocks can only measure an hour or two. They can't keep track of a whole day.

Much time flowed by before the mechanical clock was invented around the year 1090 by a Chinese astronomer. It consisted of a water clock attached to a gear driven by a weight on a rope. The weight,

Old clocks were big and beautiful, like this one in Old Town Square, in Prague, Czechoslovakia.

which dropped slowly to the ground over time, pulled the gear at a fairly even rate. By the year 1300, dropping weights powered clocks in Europe, too.

Tick tock

Early clocks were difficult to regulate. They often ran fast or slow, depending on how quickly the weights fell. By the mid-1300s, clockmakers solved this problem with a lever, which clicked in and out of the notches in a toothed wheel. The lever controlled how fast the wheel turned and caused the clock's weights to fall at a steady rate. The sound of the lever at work is the "tick-tock" in the clock.

Clocks driven by coiled springs, called mainsprings, began ticking by about 1450. As the mainspring uncoiled, it caused the gears in the clock to turn. Springs made it possible to build small, light clocks that could be used in homes. They also made watches possible, though the first watches were really just portable clocks.

Glowing Time

Some clocks and watches use Light-Emitting Diodes (LEDs) to show the time. The diodes are crystals that turn electricity into light. They glow when activated. If you have a clock radio, it is likely to display numbers using LEDs.

As time marched on, new inventions helped people keep track of it. In 1656, Dutch astronomer Christian Huygens added a pendulum to the clock. A pendulum is a weight that swings back and forth at a steady rate. A clock with a pendulum was much more accurate than one without. It also ran for a day, or even a week, without needing its spring wound or its weights adjusted. Today's grandfather clocks still use pendulums. By the early 1900s, clocks used electricity.

Wristwatches

Wristwatches became popular after World War I. American soldiers took to wearing them because it was easier to glance at a wristwatch than to fumble with a pocket watch. By 1957, people could buy watches powered by tiny batteries, instead of watches that needed winding.

Other discoveries in the 1900s made timekeeping even more accurate. In 1928, researchers found that a quartz crystal could be used as a timekeeper because it vibrated at a steady rate—exactly 32,768 times per second—when electricity flows through it. In a quartz-crystal watch, a computer chip turns these vibrations into electric pulses that move a watch's hands or change the numbers on its display.

Today, watches can do several jobs. Watches for diving record the time, water depth, and water temperature. Hiking watches tell the longitude, latitude, and altitude. Some watches even send data to a computer! *See also Calculator; Computer.* ●

COMB AND HAIRBRUSH

Drawings of prehistoric people often show them with wild, tangled hair. Some of our ancestors, though, used combs. Such combs were carved from animal bone or made from the ridged backbones of large fish. In ancient Egypt, people used ivory and wood combs with two rows of teeth both for combing hair and pinning it back. Women of ancient Rome decorated their hair with gold, silver, and jeweled combs. Tortoise shell, animal horn, and ivory from elephant tusks were also used.

Plastic combs appeared in 1862, when an English chemist named Alexander Parkes invented an early form of plastic. He used the material to make combs and other hair ornaments that looked as if they were made from ivory, which is expensive.

Hairbrushes joined combs on the bureau in the late 1700s. Early brushes were made of bristly hog hair set in a handle, just as many toothbrushes were. And, like toothbrushes, most hairbrushes began to be made with nylon bristles after nylon was invented in 1934. *See also Toothbrush.* ●

COMIC BOOK

The first comic book was published in 1934 and was called *Famous Funnies #1*. It was about the same size and shape as a modern comic book, but *Famous Funnies* was simply a collection of comic strips that had appeared in newspapers. Six months later, a comic book called *New Fun* hit the newsstands, and featured brand-new comics.

Superheroes

Then, in 1938, a superhero who had been rejected by the newspapers burst onto the scene. His name was Superman, and his adventures appeared in the first issue of *Action Comics.* Since then, the Man of Steel has inspired the creation of many other superheroes, such as Batman, Captain Marvel, and Wonder Woman. In the 1940s, comic books starring Mickey Mouse, Archie and friends, and others became wildly popular.

Today, Superman, Batman, and other superheroes, such as the Green Lantern, the X-Men, and Spider-Man, still appeal to fans, while other readers prefer the goings-on of Sabrina the Teenage Witch, Scooby Doo, Pokémon creatures, and others. Both adults and kids collect comic books, some of which sell for very high prices. ●

COMMERCIALS

Television commercials and television shows share a common history. By the late 1940s, TV sets were becoming common items in American homes. Early TV shows usually had a sponsor—a company that hosted the show and ran commercials during breaks. The commercials usually consisted of a speaker reading an announcement or a performer doing a song-and-dance routine.

Because commercials were not recorded in advance as they are today, viewers saw any mistakes that occurred, such as a dog refusing to eat the dog food being advertised. So companies began filming their commercials. Shows also began featuring ads by more than one company. Celebrities, such as movie stars, often pitched the products.

TV to advertise Planters® peanuts. The Campbell Kids® began sipping soup on TV and murmuring "M'm, m'm, good!" in 1953. The Rice Krispies Elves—Snap, Crackle, and Pop®—joined the gang in the 1950s. The Pillsbury Doughboy® first giggled on TV in the early 1960s.

TV commercials are produced by companies called advertising agencies. They work with the companies that sell the products to create ideas for commercials. The commercial first appears as a storyboard, which looks like a comic strip. After the commercial is filmed, it is shown to test audiences who give their opinions about it. Finally, the commercial airs on TV. Most commercials are 30 to 60 seconds in length. Today, the average American who watches TV regularly sees about 20,000 commercials a year. *See also Television.* ●

Animated characters

The first TV commercial starring cartoon characters was an Ajax cleanser ad that appeared in 1948. It featured three elves called the Ajax Pixies, and they sang one of the first commercial songs, called "jingles," to become popular.

Other animated characters quickly followed, and by the 1950s many of today's characters were already in business. Mr. Peanut, a dapper nut designed by a 14-year-old boy in a contest in 1916, appeared on

An animated Campbell's soup commercial began as a series of scenes, like this one, on a storyboard.

COMPACT DISC

A compact disc is a round, plastic device on which information has been recorded electronically. A layer of aluminum covers the plastic, and a layer of acrylic coats the metal to protect it. The disc's shiny underside holds the information.

A compact disc, or CD for short, that is devoted to music is called an audio CD. It is most often played on a CD player. CDs that contain software programs or combinations of words, sounds, and images (such as photographs or videos) are known as CD-ROMs. This stands for Compact Disc Read-Only Memory. "Read only" means the disc can't be recorded on anymore. CD-ROMs are placed in a computer's CD-ROM drive, which reads the information on the disc and displays it on the computer's screen. Information is stored on the CD in the form of tiny bumps and flat spaces. These bumps are so tiny that about 3 billion bumps can fit on one CD. Together, the bumps and flat spaces form an electrical code that a CD player or computer translates back into sound and light. The code is arranged in a spiral pattern on the underside of the CD. This spiral is so densely packed on the CD that it would span over 3 miles (5 km) if it were stretched out straight.

Records and audiotapes

Before compact discs were introduced in 1982, people listened to music stored on

The Super CD: DVD

In 1996, the digital video disc, or DVD, and the DVD player were first introduced to play back movies and concerts. A digital video disc is the same size as a compact disc but holds much more information. A CD-ROM can hold about 780 million "bytes" of data. A byte stands for one piece of data, such as one letter. A DVD, however, can hold 17 billion bytes of data! The reason a DVD has such a huge capacity is that data can be stored on both sides of the disk and also on a second layer that is tucked beneath the top layer. Data on a CD is stored only on one side of the disc. In addition, the bumps and spaces on a DVD are much more closely packed than on a CD, and the laser in a DVD player uses a beam with a higher power than the laser in a CD player.

records and audiotapes, often called cassettes. A record stores sound in the form of tiny bumps and dips in a thin groove that spirals around and around the record's surface. This wavy line is read by a diamond-tipped needle that runs along the groove from the outside edge of the record to the middle. The needle's vibrating motion is turned into electrical signals that are then used to produce sound. The record is played on a machine called a turntable.

The first records spun around 78 times per minute and so people called them 78s. Smaller records were called 45s. They became popular in the 1950s. Long-playing records, or LPs, first appeared in 1931 and became popular in 1948 when manufacturers began producing plastic records that did not break easily. Today, records are bought mainly by collectors.

Audiocassettes store sound on a tape that is made of plastic covered with a layer of magnetic material. Recording on tape involves using electric currents to produce changes in the positions of the magnetic material's particles. Audiocassettes, while not as popular as CDs, are still widely sold.

The CD advantage

CDs are favored by many music fans because they are free of electrical noises, such as hisses and pops, that can be heard on many records. CDs last longer because the laser beams that read them do not cause physical wear and tear on the disc, unlike the needle that reads a record or the playback heads that read an audiocassette. *See also Compact Disc Player; Computer.* ●

COMPACT DISC PLAYER

A compact disc player (CD player) is a machine that reads information stored on an audio compact disc (CD). Sound on a CD is stored as tiny bumps and flat spaces arranged in spiral grooves on the underside of a CD.

A laser beam inside the player shines on the underside of the CD as it spins, moving from the CD's center to the outer edge. A CD spins 500 times a minute at its center and 200 times a minute at the edge.

As the laser beam skims across the grooves, its light reflects off the flat areas. It does not bounce off the bumps. These on-off signals are turned into electrical pulses by a light-sensitive device called a photodiode. The CD player then turns the electrical pulses into sound. *See also Compact Disc; Computer.* ●

COMPUTER

Computers began as calculators—a word based on the Latin word *calculi,* which means "pebbles." (Merchants in ancient Rome used pebbles to add and subtract.) In 1642, a Frenchman named Blaise Pascal invented a device that could add and subtract. It used wheels with numbers on them. A German mathematician, Gottfried Wilhelm von Leibniz, improved on this in 1671 with a calculator that could also multiply and divide.

About 150 years later, Charles Babbage, British math professor, figured out that a a machine could be programmed to do calculations. In 1822, he designed a machine that used hundreds of rods and gears to

Apple's colorful iMac computers are compact, powerful, and fun. This one is connected to a digital camera.

calculate complex problems. With the help of Augusta Ada Byron, Babbage designed a second computing machine. This one would be run by steam power and programmed using cards with holes punched in them.

Babbage's ideas finally came to life in 1943 with a machine called the Harvard Mark I. It had about 3,300 switches that turned on and off as electricity ran through them. The Mark I could solve mathematical problems in four seconds or less.

From giants to midgets

Then, in 1945, the Electronic Numerical Integrator and Computer (ENIAC) came on line. Instead of switches, ENIAC used vacuum tubes, which turned on and off as electricity ran through them. ENIAC solved 5,000 addition problems in one second.

But neither machine could have fit on your desk. The Mark I weighed 5 tons and was 55 feet (16 meters) long—almost the length of two buses. ENIAC filled two rooms and had 17,468 vacuum tubes. It used more electricity in a second than a

Bits and Bytes

A computer can do very complex things, but the language it uses consists only of 0s and 1s. These simple binary numbers control the pulses of electricity in a computer: 0 is "off" and 1 is "on." When you input data, it is changed into sequences of 0s and 1s that tell the computer what to do.

A single binary number is called a bit. Eight bits in a row are called a byte. A kilobyte is 1,000 bytes (1,024 bytes, to be exact). A megabyte is one million bytes, and a gigabyte is one billion bytes. Yet the microchip that processes all this is no bigger than your fingernail!

THEN AND NOW. *In 1952, the mighty UNIVAC correctly predicted that Dwight D. Eisenhower would win the U.S. presidential election, based on just one percent of the vote. Today's computers, even super-small, hand-held ones, pack much more power than UNIVAC.*

typical family used in a week. Another early computer, UNIVAC (Universal Automatic Computer), was bigger than a two-car garage!

In 1948, an electronic device called the transistor was invented. Transistors were smaller and faster than vacuum tubes and used less electricity. In the 1970s, even smaller transistors were packed onto tiny slivers of silicon called microchips. Microchips led to the first PC (personal computer), which went on sale in 1975. It was called the Altair 8800 and was followed in 1977 by the Apple II.

Today, a microchip as small as a ladybug contains thousands, even millions, of transistors and other electronic devices. Such tiny powerhouses enable a computer no bigger than a magazine to work many times faster than the enormous ENIAC or UNIVAC of the past. Microchips also provide the power in small, hand-held computers.

Change occurs swiftly in computing— it's anyone's guess how much smaller, faster, and more powerful computers of the future will be. *See also Calculator; E-mail; Internet.* ●

COOKIE

The word *cookie* comes from a Dutch word *koekje,* meaning "little cake." If you think about it, a cookie *is* a small, flat, sweet cake.

Bakers in Europe in the 1600s tested how hot their ovens were by dropping little bits of cake dough onto pans and putting them in the ovens. The children got to eat the little cakes after they were baked.

People who came to live in the United States brought their cookie recipes from their native lands. Although there were many types of cookies, most were based on a dough made with flour, butter, sugar, and egg. The huge variety came from adding different ingredients to the basic dough and

Chocolate chip cookies

baking the cookies in different shapes.

Chocolate chips

Chocolate chip cookies were first created in the 1930s when the cook at the Toll House Inn in Massachusetts realized she was out of raisins. So she put little bits of chocolate into the cookie dough instead. The delicious treats were first known as Toll House cookies. *See also Candy; Chocolate; Doughnut.* ●

CRAYON

Most likely, the first crayon you ever used was a Crayola® crayon. Crayola® crayons are made by the Binney & Smith Company, which created the modern crayon in 1903. Back then, the company sold red barn paint, slate pencils, white chalk, and lampblack, a dark sooty powder used to make inks and paints.

Workers at the company got the idea of mixing this dark powder with wax to make a tool that could write easily on metal and glass. Colored powders, called pigments, were soon added to the wax to make colorful writing tools that were dubbed *crayons.* Alice Binney, the wife of one of the Binney & Smith partners, came up with the word *Crayola* by combining the French word *craie* (meaning "chalk") with *ola,* from *oleaginous,* which means "oily."

Animal Crackers

Animal crackers were invented in England, but became famous in the United States after 1902. In that year, the National Biscuit Company (now called Nabisco) began selling them in boxes that looked like circus wagons. A string handle made the box fun to carry. "Barnum's Animals" (a reference to the famous circus) was printed on the box. The cookies came in 18 shapes. Each box contained 22 cookies, just as today's boxes do.

How crayons are made

Making crayons involves blending wax and pigments in vats. This mixture is poured into a giant, slowly spinning mold that is full of small holes the size and shape of crayons. The wax mixture cools and hardens inside the holes. After the crayons are removed from the mold, they are wrapped in their individual, color-coordinated paper covers and boxed. Today, Binney & Smith manufactures nearly 3 billion crayons a year. *See also Pen; Pencil.* ●

DICTIONARY

A is for Akkadians, the people who made the oldest-known dictionary. The Akkadians lived in Mesopotamia, an ancient land that is now Iraq. Their dictionary is a list of words dating back to 600 B.C.

A modern dictionary, however, is more than just a list of words. It also gives the meaning of the word, tells about its history, gives examples of how it is used, and shows how to pronounce it.

Americans often refer to a dictionary known as *Webster's*. Noah Webster wrote the first American dictionary of the English language. It was called the *Compendious Dictionary of the English Language* and was published in 1806.

Half a million words!

The largest dictionary of the English language is the *Oxford English Dictionary* (OED). It was first published in its entirety in 1928 and defined 414,825 words. Each word included the story of its origin and the history of its use since the year 1150. The author of most of this first OED was a Scottish man named James Murray. He started the work in 1879. Five years later, he was only up to the word *ant!*

Today's OED defines more than 500,000 words and uses over 2 million quotations that show the histories of the words. This material fills a set of 20 books with a total of 21,730 pages. The set weighs 150 pounds (68 kg). It is also available on CD-ROM and online. *See also Book.* ●

DISHES

If prehistoric people ate from dishes, they used what nature provided: big leaves and pieces of wood. The ancient Romans often ate foods baked and served in pastry. By the Middle Ages, people put their food on thick slices of stale bread called *trenchers*. Trenchers sopped juices from food. They could then be eaten or fed to animals.

Modern china can be pretty to look at and sturdy enough to be washed in a dishwasher.

In the 1300s, people began using 12-inch square wooden trenchers with a big circular area in the center for food. A small hollowed-out hole on the rim held salt to dip meat into. Often, two people shared the same trencher.

From pewter to plastic

By the 1600s, people began using pewter plates, which were made mostly of tin. These metal plates lasted longer than wooden ones, but eventually wore out from knife marks. Wealthy people preferred ceramic plates from China.

China plates became common in the late 1700s after a British manufacturer, Josiah Wedgewood, designed a method of producing china dishes in large quantities.

Today, many people prefer unbreakable plastic dishes that can be used inside a microwave oven. *See also Silverware.* ●

DOLL

As far back as 40,000 years ago, people made tiny human figures out of clay, stone, and other materials. These figures may have looked like dolls, but they were not toys. People believed the dolls would bring them good luck, which meant the land would produce food, and women would have babies. All the while, though, children probably played with toy dolls, most likely made of sticks and rags.

Dolls through the ages

The first children known to have toy dolls lived in ancient Greece. Dolls were made of wood, clay, or cloth stuffed with straw. The dolls' hair was made of real hair or strings of clay beads. Some even had jointed legs and arms that could move. Roman boys played with soldier dolls while girls played with dolls that looked like grown women.

Simple wooden dolls with jointed limbs entertained children for centuries. By the 1600s, wooden dolls' faces were being finely carved and painted. Some dolls even had glass eyes.

By the late 1700s, dolls were made of a kind of

This GI Joe doll was based on the Tuskegee Airmen of World War II.

Dolls are more than toys. Old-fashioned costume dolls are prized by collectors.

papier-mâché and a mixture of different materials. The dolls were painted and varnished and sometimes coated in wax. Wax dolls became popular in the mid-1800s, as did stuffed dolls with heads and limbs made of china.

Homemade and plastic dolls

Most parents, however, couldn't afford such fancy dolls, so many children still cuddled homemade ones. Mothers in colonial America, for example, made dolls out of corn husks. They also stuffed scraps of material with sawdust to make rag dolls. Fathers carved wooden dolls called peg dolls or pennywoods for their children.

The first plastic dolls appeared in the late 1800s. Today, most dolls are made of a kind of plastic called vinyl.

Baby dolls

Dolls looked like children or adults until the mid-1800s when doll factories began making baby dolls.

Dolls of the 1820s were the first to have eyes that shut when they lay down to make them look as if they were sleeping. Other dolls of this period were the first to walk and talk, too. An 1827 doll could say "mama" when it was squeezed. By the late 1900s, baby dolls could not only walk and talk but also crawl, burp, eat, cry, soil their diapers, and require bandages.

One of the most popular dolls ever is the Barbie doll. Since her 1959 debut, over 500 million Barbies have been sold. Barbie has worn many different costumes and has run for president. *See Stuffed Animal.* ●

DOUGHNUT

Who invented the hole in the doughnut? Credit often goes to a young American boy, Hanson Gregory. He suggested the idea to his mother in 1847 so that the dough in her little fried cakes would cook more evenly and not be soggy in the middle. A plaque honoring his idea was attached to his home in Maine in 1947.

Doughnut holes

Fried cakes, however, had been popular for centuries in many cultures. In the 1500s, the Dutch fried little round balls of sweet dough not much bigger than walnuts. They often put a raisin or nut in the cake's center. By the 1800s, the little cakes were called *dough nuts*. Today, such little blobs of batter are called *doughnut holes*—the tiny treats fried up from the dough plucked out of the middle of doughnuts. *See also Cookie.* ●

E-MAIL

"E-mail" stands for electronic mail. It is a way of sending messages via a computer to other computer users. To send messages by e-mail, you log on to an e-mail computer program and type in an e-mail address. The address consists of a name and a destination linked by the symbol @. You then type your message into the e-mail program. Clicking your mouse or pressing a key on your keyboard sends the message on its way through the Internet.

The message arrives at a computer called a server. The server is housed at the offices of an Internet Service Provider, if the person you are writing to has such an account. Large companies may have their own servers on site. E-mail messages are stored in the server.

When you want to receive e-mails, you log on to a computer and connect with the server. The messages can then be retrieved, opened, and read or printed out—or they can be forwarded to someone else. You can also attach documents, as well as illustrations and photos, to an e-mail message. *See also Computer; Internet.* ●

The AOL welcome screen lets you send or read e-mail, enter a chat room, or explore the Internet.

ERASER

People wrote with pencils for at least 300 years before the eraser was invented. It wasn't that they didn't make mistakes. They did, and they used bread to erase them. Rubber erasers, however, had to wait for the development of rubber.

Luck and latex

Rubber is made from latex, a thick liquid that flows from certain plants when they are cut. Natives of South America knew how to make rubber and used it for shoes, water-bags, and other everyday items. But natural rubber softens and grows sticky in hot weather and cracks in cold weather.

In 1839, Charles Goodyear, an American inventor, accidentally spilled a mixture of rubber and sulfur on a hot stove and discovered how to make better rubber. Goodyear's rubber was flexible, firm, and not sticky.

Rubber erasers became part of pencils in 1858 after two Americans devised a way to glue rubber to the top of a pencil and clamped a metal ring around it. Today, most erasers are made from a mix of rubber, sulfur, vegetable oil, and a powdered stone called pumice. *See also Pencil.* ●

EYEGLASSES

Eyeglasses improve vision by bending light waves so that they are focused properly on the back of the eye. Most lenses are either convex or concave. Convex lenses bend light inward and make close-up images look bigger. People who are farsighted use convex lenses to help them see close-up items clearly. Concave lenses bend light outward and make distant objects appear in focus. Nearsighted people, who can see well up close but not at a distance, use concave lenses.

Visionaries

In A.D.1000, an Arabian scientist named Alhazen wrote that a curved lens made from a crystal made objects look bigger. About 250 years later, English scientist Roger Bacon noticed that such a lens made print on a page look bigger. By about 1280, someone in Italy—it is not known who—came up with the idea of fitting convex lenses into a frame. Early lenses were made of polished gemstones, though glass soon replaced them.

First Sunglasses

Sunglasses were used to shield eyes from sunlight long before eyeglasses were invented. By 500 B.C., the Chinese were wearing glasses that contained sheets of dark quartz crystal. The Inuits of northern Canada and Alaska blocked the glare of sun on snow by wearing wooden or bone goggles with thin slits cut in them.

In the 1300s and 1400s, people did not get prescriptions for eyeglasses. They simply tried on different pairs of glasses until they found a pair that worked. Some people who need eyeglasses today do the same thing.

Benjamin Franklin, an American statesman and scientist, put convex and concave lenses together to make the first pair of bifocals in 1784. The wearer looked through the bottom lenses to read and the top half to see distant objects. Today, bifocals have reading lenses fitted into the bottom half of the larger lens.

Keeping glasses on the nose also occupied eyeglass-wearers. At first, people held their glasses in front of their eyes. Over time, people began tying them around their heads with straps. Others looped weighted strings over their ears. In the early 1700s, eyeglasses with "temples"—side pieces that hooked over the ears—were invented in England.

By the 1900s, eye doctors could prescribe exactly the right type of lenses for their patients. Plastic frames and lenses made eyeglasses lighter and easier to wear. Plastic contact lenses, invented in the 1930s, now help 25 million Americans see more clearly. ●

FABRIC

Fabric, or cloth, is material made by weaving threads together to make clothes and other products. Threads come from plants, animals, or are made from chemicals processed in factories. The oldest fragments of fabric we have date back 18,000 years.

Wool

The hair of sheep and other woolly animals has been woven into fabric since ancient times. Wool fibers are covered with tiny scales that overlap like shingles on a roof. This helps wool shed water. Wool is especially good at keeping you warm, because its fibers trap little air pockets. Wool fibers are also curly and springy, so wool garments bounce back into shape after being worn.

Wool processing begins when a sheep's hair, called fleece, is clipped from its body. The fleece comes off in one piece, leaving the sheep with very short hair. (Like your

THEN. *The early looms that wove threads into fabric were hand-operated. Steam-powered looms were introduced as early as 1785.*

own hair after it's been cut, a sheep's fleece grows back quickly.) The fleece, however, is greasy, matted, and dirty, and must be cleaned before it can be spun into thread or woven into cloth.

Woolly Animals

Sheep are not the only animals that supply fibers for fabrics. Goats, such as the Angora and the Kashmir, grow some of the softest, most expensive wool in the world. So do camel-like animals called alpacas and vicuñas that live in parts of South America. Camels also supply wool. The giant musk oxen of northern Canada and Greenland provide a thick wool called qiviut.

Spinning wheels

Spinning wool was a slow, difficult job in ancient times. The process was transformed by the spinning wheel, which was invented in India and brought to Europe in the late 1200s. The wheel greatly sped up the task of spinning wool threads into strands that could be woven together later.

In 1766, the spinning jenny was invented in England by James Hargreaves. It did the work of eight spinning wheels at one time. Over the next 200 years, bigger and faster machines took over the job.

NOW. *Modern looms weave thousands of threads at incredibly high speeds to make wide bolts of fabric.*

Silk

An insect is the source of one of the world's finest fabrics: silk. Caterpillars called silkworms spin silken cocoons for themselves when they are ready to turn into moths. Just one cocoon contains a silk thread up to 5,000 feet (1,500 meters) long! Several threads are spun together to make a thread thick enough to be woven into fabric.

According to legend, a 14-year-old Chinese empress discovered silk about 5,000 years ago. The story may be a myth, but China ruled the silk trade in ancient times. Anyone who tried to smuggle silkworms out of China was put to death. But in A.D. 552, smugglers succeeded in sneaking silkworm eggs out of China by hiding them in hollow tubes of bamboo. Although silk industries sprang up in other countries, China is still the world's leading producer of silk.

Cotton

China is also the world's leading producer of cotton. Cotton was first woven into fabric more than 4,000 years ago in India, Peru, Mexico, Egypt, and China.

Cotton is made from fluffy fibers attached to the seeds of the cotton plant. The bundles of seeds and fibers are called bolls. Machines now harvest cotton bolls in most countries. But just 150 years ago, bolls were picked by hand. Seeds and fibers were separated by hand, too. A worker could clean only about one pound of cotton a day. Then, in 1793, an American named Eli Whitney invented the cotton gin. This machine had rollers and wire teeth to separate cotton fibers and seeds. It did the work of 50 people at once.

The cotton your jeans are made of started out in a cotton field much like this one.

Synthetics

Many of the fabrics we use today, such as rayon, nylon, acrylic, Lycra, and polyester, were invented in laboratories. These man-made fabrics are called *synthetics*. They are made by mixing chemicals together and forming threads from the mixture. The threads can then be woven into long-lasting, easy-care fabrics. *See also Plastics.* ●

FIRE TRUCK

Fire trucks are vehicles designed to fight fires. Most fire trucks are bright red, but some are yellow, green, or even purple. Different types of fire trucks handle different jobs at a fire. The two most familiar trucks are the pumper truck and the aerial, or ladder, truck.

A pumper carries its own supply of water and almost a half-mile of fire hoses, which can be hooked up to fire hydrants. Some can also shoot water from a water gun mounted on a central platform. A pumper can spray up to 1,500 gallons (5,678 liters) of water per minute. Some very powerful pumpers can shoot up to 8,000 gallons (30,284 liters) of water per minute. That's enough water to fill about 200 bathtubs.

An aerial truck lets firefighters rescue people from the upper floors of a building and to enter the building. This type of fire truck carries a high-extension ladder, ladders for use at lower levels, and fire hoses.

Other fire-fighting vehicles include the snorkel truck, "haz-mat" truck, rescue truck, and tanker truck. A snorkel truck hoists a crane containing a fire hose. This crane, which is on a turntable, can reach up and over the side of a building. It is used for rescue work and for spraying water. A "haz-mat" truck handles hazardous materials such as spilled fuel or chemicals that must be soaked up with special fabrics or, if they are burning, doused with foam instead of water. A rescue truck carries tools, ropes, and other

THEN AND NOW. *The ladder on an aerial fire truck can extend 100 feet (30 meters), reaching the sixth floor of a high-rise building. A nozzle at the ladder's end lets firefighters spray water closer to the blaze. Before the introduction of gas-powered motors and trucks, fire trucks were carriages pulled to the scene by people or galloping horses.*

equipment. A tanker truck carries water for pumpers. It is used in places lacking hydrants, such as farms in remote areas.

The first fire truck was a combination of a water pump and water tank invented in 1659 by Joseph Jencks. Firefighters pulled it to a fire, refilling it with water from leather buckets. Until the invention of fire hydrants in 1801 and fire hoses, fires were fought by "bucket brigades"—lines of people passing buckets of water from pond to fire and passing empty buckets back for refilling. ●

FLASHLIGHT

The battery-powered flashlight came to light in the 1890s— not as a tool but as an electric plant light! The first flashlight was a tube with a battery inside and a light bulb at  one end. The tube sat inside a flowerpot and could be turned on to light up the plant. John Lionel Cowen invented the tube, but he sold the idea to a Russian immigrant named Conrad Hubert.

Hubert quickly found that nobody wanted to buy his electric flowerpots. So he removed the tubes from the pots and called them "portable electric lights." These were a big hit! Based on his success, Hubert started the Eveready Flashlight Company. Today, the company is the world's biggest manufacturer of flashlights and batteries.

Modern flashlights are more powerful and come in many different shapes and sizes. But flashlights are still basically tubes with a light bulb at one end and a battery inside. *See also Battery; Light Bulb.* ●

FOOTBALL

Say "football" in many parts of the world, and people think you're talking about soccer, because football is the word they use for "soccer." The game Americans call football sprang from the English games of soccer and rugby.

The first American football games were played by college students in the late 1800s. The sport was nearly banned in 1905 because 18 players died and more were injured that year. President Theodore Roosevelt saved the game by meeting with college football coaches. New rules made the game safer. Equipment made of new materials, such as plastic helmets and shoulder pads, saved lives and prevented many injuries.

A football is an 11-inch (28 cm) oval ball with pointed ends, weighing almost one pound (0.4 kg). It's made of leather and is filled with air. It's often called a "pigskin," even though it's made from a cow's skin. A football used in a professional game may be in play for only six minutes before it is retired. *See also Baseball; Soccer.* ●

FROZEN FOOD

Imagine: meat from a woolly mammoth that has been frozen in northern lands for over 10,000 years. It was safely eaten by explorers' sled dogs after it was thawed. This shows just how effective freezing is as a way of preserving food.

Freezing preserves food by slowing down the growth of bacteria and other germs that spoil food. The Inuit people of northern Canada and Alaska have used their cold environment for centuries to freeze caribou and seal meat. The ancient Chinese stored snow in cellars 3,000 years ago to keep food cold.

Some frozen foods are a complete meal on a tray with several compartments while others contain just a single food, such as peas.

Fast freezing

Early forms of refrigeration invented in the late 1800s made shipping and selling frozen foods possible. Some of the first frozen foods, though, were not tasty. Meat was all right, but vegetables were mushy and bland.

The problem lay in how slowly the foods took to freeze. Slow freezing caused big ice crystals to form in the food, which damaged the food and let its liquid leak out.

An inventor named Clarence Birdseye observed how the Inuit people froze food quickly outdoors in the frigid Arctic air. Birdseye developed a method of "quick freezing" foods so that big ice crystals did not form in it.

During World War II, which lasted from 1939 to 1945, frozen food became more popular because canned foods were in short supply. By this time, too, a scientist named Mary Engle Pennington had improved on Birdseye's "quick freezing" by finding out how each kind of food should be processed.

By the 1940s, refrigerated trucks and train cars were transporting frozen food across the country. Grocery stores installed freezers. By the late 1950s, home "ice boxes," now called freezers, became widely available. *See also Ice Cream; Refrigerator.* ●

GARDEN

A garden is a section of ground where flowers, vegetables, fruits, or herbs are grown. Gardening is a favorite outdoor activity for many people. They enjoy growing flowers and tending vegetable gardens. Even city dwellers keep gardens. They may grow plants in pots on a window ledge or balcony. People who do not have room for a garden may rent a space in a community garden.

Some of the world's most amazing gardens grew more than 2,000 years ago. The most famous of these ancient gardens are the Hanging Gardens of Babylon, which bloomed in the dry land that is now Iraq.

These gardens grew on a series of steps called terraces. Fountains filled the air with the sound of trickling water. The ancient Aztec people of Mexico and the Inca people of Peru grew gardens on terraces and built fountains and ponds, too.

The ancient Egyptians and Romans also enjoyed beautiful gardens. Egyptian tombs contain paintings of lovely gardens surrounding temples. The Romans filled courtyards with trees and flowers. Other gardens of the time even featured mechanical singing birds and fountains that bubbled perfume.

Kitchen gardens

In China, gardens were designed to imitate natural landscapes. They were places for quiet thinking and reflecting on the beauty of nature. Benches and shelters were placed in spots where strollers could pause and enjoy the view.

One of the world's fanciest gardens dates back to the 1660s. It is known as the garden at Versailles, a palace in France. This huge garden is dotted with pools and fountains and lined with flower beds and hedges arranged carefully in patterns.

In North America, Native Americans tended gardens filled with beans, corn, and squash. European settlers likewise grew vegetables and fruit in their gardens. They also grew flowers and herbs that were used for cooking or making medicines. This kind of garden is often called a kitchen garden.

During World War II, kitchen gardens were called "victory gardens." People were encouraged to grow food in their gardens as a way of helping during wartime.

Modern gardens are filled not only with food and flowers. They also contain picnic tables and play equipment, such as play houses and swingsets, as well as birdbaths, bird feeders, stepping stones, and statues. ●

GLASS

Beads of glass were first discovered by prehistoric humans who found them in the ashes of their campfires. The beads formed when burning wood heated the sand beneath it, causing the sand to melt. The melted sand then combined with the ashes to form glass. Over time, people figured out how these beads formed. They began to make glass deliberately, using blazing fires to melt the sand and ash. These early glassmakers brushed the molten glass onto pottery as a glaze.

By 2000 B.C., glassmakers were making glass beads and even tinting them with colors. The beads were often used as money. Wealthy Egyptians wore glass beads as jewelry.

Useful glass

Around 1500 B.C., glassmakers learned how to make glass bottles and other containers. First, the glassmaker attached a little sandbag or a mold made of clay or animal dung to the end of a metal pole. He then wrapped coils of molten (melted) glass around

A drinking glass is one of the most common glass objects in our lives.

the mold and rolled it on a flat stone to smooth and shape it. When the glass cooled, the mold was removed and the bottle was ready to use.

A glassblower needs strong arms and strong lungs to turn molten (melted) glass into beautiful glass pieces.

Blowing glass

Glassmakers in Syria discovered, perhaps by accident, that one could blow into a metal tube and inflate molten glass like a bubble. This was a much easier way to form glass bottles. They also discovered that molten glass could be pulled into different shapes to make handles, spouts, and other features. Roman glassmakers used the glassblowing method to make drinking cups, among other items.

Making windows

Glass was used to make windows as far back as 400 B.C. Glassmakers poured thin sheets of molten glass, then used rough materials like sand to grind and polish them once they cooled. After the discovery of glassblowing, a new way of making windows was developed. Glassmakers blew

Glass windows add beauty and light to modern homes.

molten glass into a big bubble, then swung, twisted, and pulled it until it took on the shape of a tube. The hollow tube was then split in half and flattened.

By A.D. 1400, many large European churches had colorful stained-glass windows. Wealthy people soon began installing glass windows in their homes. By the 1600s, glass windows were more common in ordinary people's homes, as were drinking glasses.

Modern glassmaking

Today, glass is made by heating silica sand, sodium carbonate (soda ash), and limestone in huge tanks at a temperature of 2,400°F (1,300°C). Ordinary bottles and jars are still made by the glassblowing method, but the blowing is done by machines in factories.

However, the art of glassblowing by hand still exists. Glass artists use the technique to make sculptures, plates, and many other beautiful objects.

Pigments can be added to glass to give it color. Lead is added to molten glass to make lead crystal, a heavy kind of glass used to make pitchers, bowls, vases, and wine glasses. Borax is added to glass that will be made into cookware and test tubes—items that are heated frequently.

Safety glass

Car and airplane windows are made of glass that is stronger than the glass used for windows in houses. They are made by heating glass to extremely high temperatures and sandwiching plastic between the glass panes so they don't shatter into sharp-edged pieces. ●

Glass Boats

It may seem strange to you, but glass is used to make cars, boats, curtains, and other fabrics. This kind of glass is called fiberglass. It is light, strong, and won't rust or rot in water.

Fiberglass is made by pressing molten (melted) glass through a plate filled with little holes to make long, flexible strings of glass that may stretch as long as a mile (1.6 km). It is then woven like fabric and mixed with plastic to make a material that can be molded into a car body or a boat.

Fiberglass also holds in heat and so is used in heavy drapes and as insulation stuffed into the walls of buildings.

GREETING CARD

The custom of sending greeting cards on special occasions seems to date back to the origins of Valentine's Day. In ancient Rome,

a festival in mid-February was held every year to celebrate the courting and mating of young men and young women. Sending love letters became a traditional part of the celebration. The holiday became known as Valentine's Day hundreds of years later.

By the 1300s, people across Europe were sending fond notes on Valentine's Day. The oldest surviving Valentine's card was written in 1415 by a Frenchman named Charles, Duke of Orléans, while he was imprisoned in the Tower of London. He wrote the note to his wife.

Commercial cards

Most people continued to write their own cards in the centuries that followed. Machine-printed cards didn't become popular until the late 1700s. Many were blank inside, so people could still handwrite their messages. The first commercial Christmas card was made in London in 1843. Today, the most popular holiday cards are Christmas cards.

The most popular non-holiday card, however, is the birthday card. Over half of all non-holiday cards are birthday cards. Many people now use computers to make their own cards or to send electronic greeting cards via e-mail. ●

GUM

Chewing gum is made from a mixture of materials called latexes. Latex is a gummy liquid produced by certain kinds of tropical trees, such as the rubber tree. It oozes out of the tree when its bark is cut. Some types of latex in gum are synthetics, which means they are made from chemicals that are similar to natural substances.

Latex from gum trees is one of the ingredients used to make chewing gum.

Chewing gum also contains softeners to help keep gum moist. Softeners are usually different kinds of vegetable oils. Gum is sweet because it contains sugar and corn syrup or artificial sweeteners. The gum's taste comes from flavorings, such as peppermint, spearmint, and cinnamon.

Bubble blowers

Bubble gum is a mixture of gum ingredients that can be blown into big bubbles. Bubble gum companies keep their special mixes a secret. The first bubble gum bubble popped in 1906. This gum, called

Blibber-Blubber, was invented by an American named Frank Henry Fleer. Unfortunately, Blibber-Blubber stuck tight to the face after popping. It was not until 1928 that a Fleer Corporation worker named Walter Diemer invented a bubble gum that peeled off the face easily. This gum, called Double Bubble, became an instant hit.

Liking to chew is not new

Chewing gum is an old human habit. The Inuit people of northern Canada and Alaska chewed on raw whale skin and blubber since ancient times. People in northern Europe chewed a gummy liquid that oozed from birches and spruce trees as far back as 9,000 years ago. Central American Indians, such as the Maya and Aztec, chewed a tree gum called chicle centuries ago. Chicle was the latex first used to make chewing gum in 1869. ●

HAMBURGER

A hamburger is made of ground-up beef pressed and formed into a round shape, called a patty. Hamburgers are very popular in the United States. Americans eat more than 5 billion hamburgers a year in restaurants alone. The hamburger's popularity began in the 1920s, when White Castle and other hamburger restaurants popped up alongside newly built roads and highways. In 1955, McDonald's® joined the scene.

The hamburger has always been a popular take-out food. The first burger was eaten long ago by people living in Central Asia who wandered across the plains with their herds of cattle. These people, called Tartars, first made the meat more soft and tender by putting big pieces of it under their horses' saddles. After a long day's riding, the Tartars removed the meat, shredded it, and mixed it with onions and spices. Then they ate it raw.

Hamburg steaks

The dish, called Tartar steak, found its way to Germany at least 600 years ago. There, it was named *Hamburg steak* after the German city of Hamburg, and was eaten raw or cooked. German immigrants brought the dish to the United States in the 1800s. Over time, it became known as *hamburger steak*, then *hamburger*, and finally just *burger*.

Another type of hamburger is the *Salisbury steak*. It is named after Dr. J.H. Salisbury, an English doctor, who began praising shredded beef as a health food in 1888.

No one is sure just who first thought of putting burgers on buns. Today, people eat burgers not only on buns but also piled high with pickles, tomatoes, cheese, and other fixings.

See also Hot Dog; Restaurant. ●

53

Hockey

Field hockey is a game in which teams of players drive a ball across a field using sticks. A team scores by hitting the ball into the other team's goal. Each team has 11 players. The hard ball is about the size of a baseball.

The ancient Egyptians played a game similar to hockey about 4,000 years ago. The ancient Greeks, Romans, and Persians played hockey, too.

People living in parts of Great Britain also played hockey-like games. It was in Britain that field hockey became an organized game with international rules. The name, however, comes from a French word, *hoquet*, which means "hooked stick."

Hockey on ice

Ice hockey is based on field hockey. It is played on ice in a rink by two teams of six players each. Players wear ice skates and protective gear. Instead of a ball, ice-hockey players hit a round disc called a puck. The hard rubber puck is 3 inches (7.6 cm) wide and 1 inch (2.5 cm) thick.

Ice hockey got its start in Canada in the mid-1800s. It was played by British soldiers working there. To pass the time in winter, they began playing field hockey on ice, wearing skates. By 1855, ice hockey had rules much like the ones used today. *See also Baseball; Football; Ice Skating; Soccer.* ●

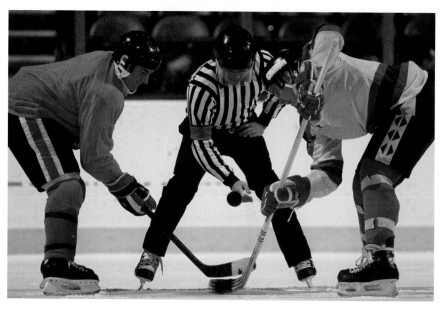

Opposing players try to gain control of the puck at the start of a hockey game. A puck hit by a hockey stick can zoom up to 100 miles (160 km) per hour.

Hot dog

A hot dog, also called a frankfurter, is a kind of sausage. Sausages are made of ground meat mixed with spices and stuffed into a kind of skin called a casing.

People have made sausages for more than 5,000 years. Sausages are made from leftover pieces of meat mixed together. Sausages can last a long time without going bad if they are dried or smoked or if lots of salt is added to the meat.

The frankfurter is named after the city of Frankfurt in Germany. Butchers there came up with the recipe for it in 1852. Frankfurters began to be sold in the United States by the late 1800s.

The frankfurter looks a lot like the long, skinny German dog called the dachshund. As a result, sausage sellers at American fairs and baseball games

sometimes called it a "dachshund sausage." In 1906, Tad Dorgan, a cartoonist, drew a picture of a dachshund in a bun covered with mustard. According to legend, he could not spell *dachshund*, so he labeled his picture *hot dog*. The name stuck. Today, hot dogs are so popular that Americans eat over 16 billion of them a year. *See also Hamburger.* ●

ICE CREAM

Ice cream is made by stirring cream or milk with sweeteners, such as sugar or honey, and freezing it. Chocolate, vanilla, nuts, or other ingredients can also be mixed in.

The ancient Chinese ate similar desserts made of fruit juice, milk, and snow. By 1560, people in Italy enjoyed a frozen milk-and-honey dish called "flower of milk" or "cream." Nobles at a feast given by King Charles I of England in 1640 ate "cream ice." According to legend, the king liked ice cream so much that he paid his chef to keep the recipe a secret. After the king's death, the chef sold the recipe. Ice cream was no longer a state secret.

Ice cream became very popular in the United States by the 1770s. The first U.S. president, George Washington, was especially fond of it.

Ice cream for everyone

Ice cream used to be expensive, because it was hard to make. It was stirred by hand in a pot surrounded by salt and ice. While the ice cream was stirred, the pot had to be shaken.

In 1846, an American named Nancy Johnson invented a better ice-cream maker. It had an attached crank for stirring the ice cream. Then, a milk seller in Maryland, Jacob Fussell, started the first ice cream factory in 1851. By the early 1900s, new technology and methods of freezing food made it easier to make and ship ice cream.

Cones to the rescue

People first licked ice cream cones at the World's Fair in St. Louis, Missouri in 1904. According to one version of the story, an ice cream stand ran out of dishes. A pastry chef at a nearby stand came to the rescue with thin waffles folded into cones in which to place the scoops of ice cream. Today, ice cream comes in an incredible array of flavors—yet vanilla remains the nation's favorite. Americans are the world's biggest consumers of ice cream. The average American eats about 23 quarts of ice cream a year. *See also Chocolate; Frozen Food.* ●

ICE SKATES

People in cold, northern lands, such as Scandinavia, used ice skates over 2,000 years ago. These first skates had blades made out of reindeer, cattle, and elk bones. Skaters strapped the bone blades to their feet and used short poles to push themselves across ice and snow.

About 900 years ago, people in places south of Scandinavia began skating, too. In the Netherlands, people skated along frozen waterways to travel in winter. People also skated simply for fun.

Sport skating

By the late 1300s, many people wore skates made of an iron blade that fit into a slot on the bottom of a wooden shoe. In 1848, an American named E. W. Bushnell invented iron skates that clamped onto boots.

Racing on skates became an official sport called speed skating in the early 1800s in the Netherlands. Later that century, figure skating got its start when an American dancing instructor named Jackson Haines taught people to dance on ice. Today, both speed skating and figure skating are popular Olympic sports. *See also Hockey.* ●

INTERNET

The Internet is a system that links computer networks worldwide. A computer user connects to the Internet via an Internet Service Provider, such as American Online, which in turn is hooked up to the Internet.

The Internet got its start as a U.S. Defense Department network called ARPAnet, which stands for Advanced Research Projects Agency Network. ARPAnet was designed to be a computer system that would allow messages to get through even if a war knocked out telephones, TV and radio stations, and other communication systems.

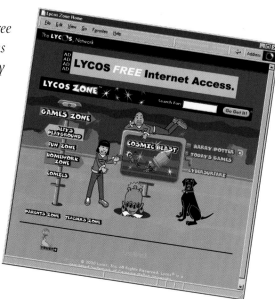

The Lycos Free Internet Access site is specially designed to help kids explore a world of fun and knowledge on the Internet.

New networks

ARPAnet was first hooked up in 1969. It linked four universities. People using ARPAnet soon began sending each other messages and documents. The National Science Foundation also set up a network called the NSFNet. Other networks began appearing, too. Within a few years, a system for sending and receiving messages was developed that could be used on all networks. By 1983, these networks were being called the Internet.

WWW.

In 1989, a researcher named Tim Berners-Lee developed a way of connecting all the different programs used on the Internet. His software was called the World Wide Web. Using this software, a person could easily jump from place to place on the Internet.

Each place, or site, on the web has its own address, called a URL (Uniform Resource Locator). To get to a website, a user simply types in the site's URL or uses a search engine to help find it.

Other software programs let people listen to music and see illustrations and videos as well as read text. By the year 2000, millions of people worldwide were using the World Wide Web to access millions of websites. People also use the Internet to play games, find information, buy products, or send e-mail messages. *See also Computer; E-mail.* ●

JEANS

Jeans are pants made out of a cotton material called denim. They first became wildly popular in the United States and later around the world.

The word *jeans* dates back to the mid-1500s. At that time, sailors from the city of Genoa in Italy wore cotton pants. The city and its sailors were known as "Gênes" in France, and so were their pants.

In 1853, an American named Levi Strauss traveled to California to seek his fortune during the gold rush. Although Strauss planned to strike gold, he also brought along rolls of canvas to sell. He thought the miners would use it for tents and mats. When he heard miners complain about the holes in their pants, Strauss got an idea. He began sewing the canvas into tough pants. The brown canvas pants were bestsellers.

Jean fashions

Miners began seeking out Strauss to buy "Levi's pants," even after he switched to using blue denim. In 1873, metal rivets (bolts) were added to the pants to make the edges of pockets stronger. Today, Levi Strauss & Company still makes jeans, which many people call Levi's®.

Basic jeans have remained popular for over 125 years. But variations on the basic style go in and out of fashion. Wide-legged jeans called "bell bottoms" were in fashion in the early 1970s, but later in the decade, many people wore skin-tight jeans. At the end of the twentieth century, jeans were very baggy. *See also Fabric.* ●

JET PLANE

The first plane flight lasted a mere 12 seconds. *Flyer 1,* built by Wilbur and Orville Wright, made this quick but historic journey on December 14, 1903. (*Flyer 1* was later renamed *Kitty Hawk.*) It set in motion a century of flight, starting with propeller planes and ending with spaceships. In between came the invention of the jet engine.

Passenger jets began flying regularly across the United States and the Atlantic Ocean in 1958.

How a jet engine works

A jet engine is a giant tube with a series of blades inside it. A fan at the front spins and sucks air into the engine. This air is squeezed, or compressed, as it travels through the series of blades. As the air is squeezed, it gets hotter—just as a bicycle tire heats up as you pump air into it.

The hot air then enters a combustion chamber. Fuel is sprayed into this chamber and ignites when it hits the hot air. The burning fuel forces hot gases out of a nozzle at the back of the engine. This fast-moving river of gas then pushes the jet forward.

The first jet engines roared to life in Germany in 1939 and were used by the military. By 1942, German bombers were flying up to 100 miles (160 km) per hour, much faster than any propeller plane.

Today, the Concorde, a sleek jet plane, flies at speeds up to 1,320 miles (2,125 km) per hour. That is twice the speed of sound. ●

JEWELRY

People have adorned themselves with jewelry for tens of thousands of years. The most common types of jewelry worn throughout history are those still used today—necklaces, rings, bracelets, pins, and earrings. Jewelry has been made out of all kinds of materials, including animal teeth, bone, leather, ivory, pearls, shells, feathers, wood, gold, silver, and precious gemstones.

The power of jewelry

Ancient peoples wore jewelry not only for decoration but also for protection from sickness and evil spirits. The ancient Greeks believed that rubies could protect their homes and farms against storms. The Zuñi Indians of the southwestern United States adorned doorways and cradles with turquoise to ward off evil spirits.

Since ancient times, jewelry has represented wealth and status. Both the ancient Chinese and the Mayans of Mexico and Guatemala considered jade to be a symbol of a person's high status or importance. Ancient Rome had laws restricting who could wear ropes of pearls. Europeans from the 1500s onward prized precious gemstones, such as emeralds and diamonds, as symbols of wealth and power.

Gold and silver

Gold has long been treasured as a metal for making jewelry not only because of its brightness but also because it does not tarnish and is easily worked. Heated gold can be hammered into thin sheets, pulled into thin wires, and bent into fancy shapes. People began working with gold as far back as 3500 B.C.

Gold jewelry, however, is not usually made of pure gold, because pure gold is very soft. Instead, gold is combined with silver, copper, and nickel to produce metal for jewelry making. Some jewelry looks like it is made of gold, but only thin sheets of gold are painted on the outside over other metals that are underneath.

Silver is another rare metal that is often used for jewelry. Like gold, silver is mixed with other metals for jewelry making. If the mixture contains a certain amount of pure silver, it is called sterling silver.

Today, most jewelry is produced in factories rather than being handmade as it was in earlier times. But some artists still craft one-of-kind pieces of jewelry by hand. Costume jewelry is made with inexpensive materials, such as plastic. Some gems imitate those used in more valuable jewelry. Zircon, for example, looks like a diamond, but it is a mineral that is not nearly as rare. ●

KEY

A key is a device that opens a lock. Keys are made so that they fit certain locks, and those locks open only for those keys. The lock in a typical front-door doorknob is known as a pin-tumbler lock, or Yale lock. It is named after Linus Yale, who invented it in 1848.

Locks and keys have been used since at least 2000 B.C. Early locks used wooden pins that fell into slots and held bolts in place. Matching keys were pushed into the lock and pushed the pins upward. If the ridges of the key matched the placement of the pins, the key lifted the pins and the lock could be opened. ●

KITCHEN

A kitchen is a room in which food is cooked. Throughout history, a kitchen held a big cooking fire. This fire usually burned inside a large stone or brick fireplace called a hearth. Food was cooked in pots and pans held over the flames. It could also be tucked into openings built into the stone or brick surrounding the fire.

About 1,400 years ago, cooks added a device called the turnspit to their hearths. A turnspit is a rod that is pushed through a piece of meat and then turned as the meat cooks over a fire. The spit had to be turned by hand.

Cooking hearths were at the heart of homes built by American colonists in the 1700s. The hearth held a wooden pole on which pots and kettles were hung. These pots were heavy—an empty one could weigh up to 40 pounds (18 kg)! Later, the pole was replaced by iron cranes that could be swung out like a gate. After hanging pots on it, the cook swung the crane back over the fire.

In front of the fire sat a "roasting kitchen" for cooking meat. This device looked like half an oil drum set on its side, with its open end facing the fire. A turnspit ran across it. Bread and other foods were baked in an oven in the side of the hearth.

The modern kitchen

In the early 1800s, cast-iron stoves began appearing in American kitchens. Kitchens in this period also had sinks made of iron or stone, which were filled with water brought into the house from a well or from a river or lake. Some people had hand pumps or

wind-powered pumps that pumped water into the sink. Pipes carried used water out of the house.

Kitchens in the early 1900s featured porcelain sinks as well as newer versions of the cast-iron stove. Refrigerators, called "iceboxes," also became standard kitchen equipment. Many kitchens contained big cabinets that included a work surface as well as drawers and shelves. These cabinets were called "hoosiers."

Electrical appliances also began appearing in the kitchens of the early 1900s. By 1920, toasters, waffle irons, and electric mixers were common. Today, most kitchens also feature garbage disposals, microwave ovens, food processors, and dishwashers. Some have a television and a computer. *See also Microwave Oven; Oven; Refrigerator.* ●

KITE

Kites first flew in China about 4,000 years ago. But no one is quite sure just how or why the ancient Chinese began flying kites. Some say kites were designed to scare away evil spirits. Others suggest that kites were flown as banners by rulers.

The uses of kites

European explorers brought kites back with them from their travels to other parts of the world. Although kites became popular toys in the 1600s, scientists later used them as tools in experiments.

In the mid-1700s, scientists flew kites with thermometers attached to them to

measure air temperatures at high altitudes. In 1752, Benjamin Franklin flew a kite with a key attached to it in order to prove that lightning was the same as electricity.

Kites have also been used in warfare. The Maori people of New Zealand flew kites with burning wood attached to them to frighten enemies. About 900 years ago in Korea, soldiers attached to kites jumped off cliffs onto the enemy below. The U.S. Army flew kites in 1898 to spy on enemy troops during the Spanish-American War.

Kites have played a more peaceful role in the sacred rituals of many Asian cultures. In China, kites symbolize good luck. In Japan, kites are flown on Children's Day, May 5, to honor boys and girls. ●

LIBRARY

The first libraries were set up over 4,000 years ago. Ancient libraries in Mesopotamia (now Iraq) held clay tablets etched with an early kind of writing called cuneiform. Ancient Roman and Greek libraries held scrolls—rolled-up sheets of paper made from the papyrus plant. The scrolls contained information about science, geography, mathematics, myths, and legends.

Rival libraries

The greatest ancient Greek library was located in Alexandria, Egypt. It stored 700,000 scrolls. Another great library existed in Pergamum, a city in what is now Turkey. The king of Egypt saw this library as a rival. He stopped shipping papyrus to Pergamum around 200 B.C. so that it would not have paper for scrolls. Librarians in Pergamum solved the problem by inventing parchment, a material made from very thin pieces of animal skin that can be written upon.

The development of the printing press around 1450 made books easier and cheaper to produce. As a result, the number of libraries grew. Many wealthy Europeans kept private libraries at home. By the 1600s, Europe had a few public libraries, too.

The first library in the United States was founded in 1638 at Harvard College in Cambridge, Massachusetts. It held 380 books. Today, the Harvard Library has more than 4 million volumes.

At first, people were allowed to read books only inside the library. Benjamin Franklin changed this practice by creating a "subscription library," which people could join by paying a small fee. The money was used to buy books that subscribers could then borrow.

The first free public library opened in 1833 in Peterborough, New Hampshire. In the late 1800s, Andrew Carnegie, a wealthy businessman, donated millions of dollars to build free libraries all across America.

Today, libraries hold not only books but also videos, CD-ROMs, newspapers and magazines, maps, and other items.

The largest library in the United States is also the largest library in the world: the Library of Congress in Washington, D.C. It holds about 119 million items, which take up about 530 miles (853 km) of bookshelves. *See also Alphabet; Book; Paper.* ●

At today's public libraries, you can read a book, look up information on the Internet, and have fun, too.

LIGHT BULB

An incandescent light bulb is a glass ball that contains a thin, coiled wire strung between two wire posts. This wire is called a filament and is made of a metal called tungsten.

When electricity flows through the filament, it heats up and glows. Tungsten is perfect for the job because it has the highest melting point of any metal.

The invention of the incandescent light bulb came after decades of work by many people. In the early 1800s, scientists found that strips of metal glowed when they were heated by electricity. Over the next few decades, they tried heating strips of carbon and a metal called platinum inside balls of glass. Some scientists found that platinum strips lasted longer if much of the air was sucked out of the glass ball. Air contains oxygen, which damages metals by reacting with them.

In 1865, a vacuum pump was invented that could suck almost all the air out of a container. Thanks to this invention, a British inventor named Joseph Swan was able to produce a light bulb with a carbon filament inside a nearly airless glass ball in 1878.

At the same time, the great American inventor Thomas Alva Edison made a light bulb with a carbon cotton filament that shone for 40 hours—longer than Swan's bulbs. Edison patented his light bulb in 1879.

Watt energy

The energy used by an incandescent bulb is measured in watts. A 100-watt bulb is brighter than a 25-watt bulb. The 25-watt bulb, though, may burn for up to 2,500 hours while the 100-watt bulb may burn out after 750 hours.

But incandescent bulbs are not energy efficient. They turn only about 8 percent of the energy they use into light. The rest is given off as heat. Other types of light bulbs, such as fluorescent bulbs, are more energy efficient. They require less energy and last longer. ●

Mail

Mail consists of all the postcards, letters, magazines, catalogs, boxes, and other items that are carried by a postal service. In the United States, postal workers deliver over 600 million pieces of mail a day to homes and businesses.

Each piece of mail starts its journey in a mailbox or mailroom. Postal workers pick up the mail and deliver it to a local post office. There the mail is put into trays and carts and shipped to a much larger postal plant for sorting.

Scanning and sorting

At the postal plant, computerized equipment processes the mail. First, the mail is poured onto conveyor belts. Machines line up the envelopes so that they all face the same way, with the stamps located in the upper right-hand corner. Another machine marks the stamps with lines. This is called "canceling." A canceled stamp cannot be used again. The piece of mail is also stamped with a postmark, a symbol that indicates the date and place it was canceled.

Next, the mail is sorted. Envelopes fly past a machine that scans the address and turns it into a bar code—a series of little lines. Other machines read the bar codes and sort the mail into groups according to their destinations around the country and

around the world. Items that cannot be scanned by machine are sorted by postal workers according to ZIP codes. ZIP stands for Zoning Improvement Plan.

The sorted mail is then shipped again. Trucks take local mail to local post offices. Airplanes and trains carry the rest to distant postal facilities. There it is sorted again for local distribution by mail carriers.

Mail carriers in olden times

Modern postal systems have ancient origins. Clay tablets in clay envelopes were carried by runners 4,000 years ago in ancient Egypt, Turkey, and other lands. Chinese rulers used a postal system 3,000 years ago. Ancient Greece and Rome boasted efficient postal systems, too. These early mail systems were used mainly by government and religious officials as well as merchants.

The first adhesive postage stamp was introduced in 1840. It was invented by Rowland Hill, an Englishman. Hill also came up with the idea that the cost of mailing a letter should be based on its weight and destination.

Over the centuries, new means of transportation have sped up the delivery of mail. Mail in ancient Greece was carried by runners. Relay runners also delivered messages in ancient India. The ancient Romans used horse-drawn coaches. Riders on horseback have galloped across Australia, India, and other countries to deliver the mail, as did Pony Express riders in the United States from 1860 to 1861. Bicycles, oxen, camels, reindeer, dog sleds, and pigeons have all carried mail. *See also E-mail.* ●

Mall

A mall is a shopping complex made up of stores lined up next to each other, designed for strolling shoppers. Most malls have one or more big department stores as well as a variety of small stores and places to eat. A mall is often enclosed so that it is shielded from the weather.

The Country Club Plaza in Kansas City, Missouri, is often considered to be the first shopping mall in the United States. It opened in 1922. Other malls and shopping centers also claim to be the nation's first.

The first fully enclosed mall was Southdale Center in Edina, Minnesota, a suburb of Minneapolis. It opened in 1956. Its original building plans included a landing pad for helicopters so that customers could be flown in from Minneapolis.

The idea of clustering sellers in one place is not new. Marketplaces have existed for thousands of years. Five thousand years ago, people in Sumeria (now Iraq) gathered in markets to buy, sell, and swap goods. Ever since, people around the world have enjoyed visiting bustling marketplaces.

The West Edmonton Mall, in Alberta, Canada, is the world's largest mall. It includes more than 800 stores, more than 100 eating places, the world's biggest indoor amusement park, a 5-acre indoor waterpark, and four submarines in an artificial lake.

The Mall of America, in Bloomington, Minnesota, is the biggest mall in the United States. It contains more than 500 stores, a roller coaster, and an aquarium. ●

A shopping mall in Jersey City, New Jersey.

Microwave oven

A microwave oven heats food by making water molecules in the food vibrate. The vibrating water molecules produce heat. This heat, in turn, heats up other kinds of molecules around them. In this way, the entire food item gets cooked.

Microwaves are a kind of energy called electromagnetic radiation. Other kinds of energy are light rays, radio waves, and X rays.

Corn kernels that unexpectedly popped were a clue to discovering that microwaves can cook food.

Radar ranges

Researchers discovered the cooking power of microwaves while experimenting with radar during World War II. Radar systems find airplanes and ships by sending out microwaves. Like echoes, the microwaves bounce off their targets and are picked up again by the radar. One day, a British physicist noticed that a bag of corn popped when it was near a magnetron, a device that produces microwaves. Another discovery was made in 1945 when an American technician, Percy Spencer, found that a nearby magnetron had melted a chocolate bar in his pocket.

Spencer worked for the Raytheon Manufacturing Company. His observation led the company to develop the first microwave oven for use in homes. It was named a Radarange®.

Today, two out of three homes have a microwave oven in the kitchen in addition to a regular oven. *See also Oven.* ●

Milk

Milk is a highly nutritious liquid food produced by mammals for their young. It is rich in protein and contains calcium and phosphorus, two minerals that are important for nutrition and growth.

The most commonly consumed milk that is commercially produced is the milk made by cows. A dairy cow is milked with a special milking machine twice a day—once in the early morning and again toward evening. The average cow can produce about 10 gallons (38 liters) a day—which is about 50 pounds (22 kg) of milk.

Doings at the dairy

The milk then goes to a dairy to be processed. There it is tested, homogenized, pasteurized, and packaged into containers. Homogenizing is the process of mixing the milk so that the rich fat in it, called butterfat, is broken into small pieces. This prevents the butterfat from separating out of the milk and rising to the top.

Pasteurizing is the process of heating milk quickly, then cooling it. This process kills disease-causing germs that may be in the milk.

Milk is used to make other products, such as cheese, butter, yogurt, and ice cream. Some or all of the butterfat can also be removed from milk in order to make 2 percent, 1 percent, and skim or nonfat milk.

Milk from other animals

Cows were not the first animals milked by

humans. Prehistoric people first milked sheep and goats about 11,000 years ago. They also milked horses and donkeys. Cattle began to be tamed at least 8,000 years ago. Pictures from Egyptian tombs dating back to 2050 B.C. show cows being milked. Goats and sheep are still milked today, and in some countries, yaks and reindeer are the main providers of milk. ●

MIRROR

A mirror is a surface that reflects light, forming an image. A still pond or even a puddle can be a mirror. A polished piece of metal or a sheet of glossy rock can also serve as a mirror.

The first mirrors made by people were simple looking-glasses, or hand mirrors. About 7,000 years ago, people in Italy and the Middle East made mirrors by polishing slabs of obsidian, a glossy black volcanic rock. Later, mirrors were made by polishing a piece of metal, such as bronze or brass, until it was smooth and shiny, and the person could see his or her reflection in it.

Silver and glass

By the Middle Ages (about A.D. 500-1500), people were making mirrors much the way we do today. A piece of glass was lined on one side with a thin sheet of metal, such as silver. In 1835, a German scientist figured out a way of bonding, or attaching, silver to glass. This process is called silvering. It is still used for producing looking-glass mirrors today. Scientific mirrors, such as the ones used in telescopes, are made by a different process.

Mirrors are usually flat, like a mirror on a wall. But some mirrors, such as shaving and makeup mirrors, have surfaces that cup inward so that they magnify images. Funhouse mirrors have warped surfaces that distort reflections. *See also Glass.*●

MONEY

Penny

Nickel

Quarter

Dime

Money is anything that is used by people to buy and sell goods. It is an item that people have agreed to give a value or worth.

People began to use money thousands of years ago. Money took many forms. A list of items used as money throughout history is long and includes pebbles, shells, beads, barley grains, tea leaves, feathers, fabrics, animal teeth, salt, spades, cattle, horses, pigs, and beetle legs! Early American colonists often used tobacco leaves as money.

Origin of coins

Of course, precious metals were also used as money. The Sumerians of the Middle East used chunks of silver as money as far back as the year 4000 B.C. These chunks were called ingots. Other ingots contained gold as well as silver, or were made of bronze. The Sumerians stamped each ingot with a seal that described what kinds of metal were in it, as well as its weight.

Weight was a very important feature of this kind of money. The value of the ingot lay in the amount of precious metal in it. A dishonest person could make an ingot that did not really contain as much metal as its seal claimed it did. People who accepted ingots as money often weighed them, just to make sure they weren't being cheated.

Making ingots led to the invention of coins. A coin is a metal object marked with symbols that show it is money. The first coins were made, or minted, about 2,700 years ago by people in the ancient land of Lydia. Lydia was a kingdom in what is today the country of Turkey. Lydian coins were made of a metal called electrum, which contains both gold and silver.

Electrum was easy to hammer and shape. The Lydians turned it into small, nut-shaped coins stamped with a picture of a lion. The amount of precious metal in each coin as well as the coin's size still counted toward its worth. The king of Lydia guaranteed the coins' value, so people gradually stopped weighing them.

Dishonest people, however, carved bits of metal off the edges of these coins. They also shook coins in a bag for hours at a time to shave some metal off of them. This reduced the value of the coins while providing the person with bits of metal

Cotton Money

Have you ever wondered why the texture of a dollar bill feels a little different than paper? That's because paper money is made mostly of cotton and some linen, which are fabrics. Regular paper is made from wood pulp.

Plastic threads run through our paper money, too. These threads help identify paper money as being real. They make it difficult for people to make fake, or counterfeit, bills.

to sell. The solution to this problem was invented in the late 1600s, when coin makers began putting a series of notches around the edges of coins. The process is called "milling." These lines are still used on dimes and quarters today. You can see the lines for yourself!

The Chinese were the first to use paper money about 2,000 years ago. This is not surprising because paper was invented in China at about the same time. However, the Chinese kept paper a secret from the rest of the world for hundreds of years. Today, paper money is sometimes known as bank notes.

Bank notes, such as dollar bills, are made by the U.S. Bureau of Engraving and Printing. One-dollar bills get the most use and begin to wear out after 18 months. Unlike worn-out coins, which are melted down and recycled, old bills are destroyed.

coins are pennies. A penny is made of zinc covered with copper. Nickels, dimes, quarters, half-dollars, and dollars are made of a mixture of nickel and copper. The gold-colored dollar coin issued in 2000 features the Native American woman Sacagawea and is made of copper and manganese-brass.

The U.S. Bureau of Engraving and Printing in Washington, D.C. produces U.S. paper money. There's a factory in Fort Worth, Texas, that also makes bills. The bureau prints up to 37 million notes a day—most of these are $1 and $20 bills to replace torn or tattered ones. In 1999, over three billion $1 bills and over four billion $20 bills were printed. *See also Paper.* ●

Making money

In the modern world, manufacturing coins and notes is handled by a nation's government.

In the United States, the U.S. Mint produces the nation's circulating coins at two plants—one in Philadelphia, Pennsylvania, and the other in Denver, Colorado. They mint over 20 billion coins a year. Over 11 billion of these

Huge machines at the U.S. Mint are used to make coins. It's a seven-step job: from punching out round discs, called blanks, to final counting and bagging.

Movie

A movie is a series of photographs that flash by so quickly that you see them as a nonstop stream of motion. Each image is called a frame. Just one second of film contains 24 frames.

The first moving pictures, however, were not films shown on a screen. They were toys used in the 1800s that could be twirled to make little pictures appear to move. People in the 1800s also enjoyed looking at pictures projected on a wall or screen by a magic lantern. A magic lantern was a device with a candle inside it. The candle light beamed through glass strips with pictures painted on them. Next, the light shone through a lens, which focused the picture on a screen.

Cameramen film from many places, including high platforms like this one.

Movie pioneers

An early pioneer of motion pictures was the British photographer Eadweard Muybridge. In 1878, he photographed for the first time the motion of an object moving quickly—in this case, a race horse. To shoot the pictures, Muybridge set up 12 cameras along a track. He attached a thin thread to each camera and strung the threads across the track. As the horse ran by, its legs broke the threads and clicked the cameras. Muybridge's cameras snapped the pictures quickly so that the images were sharp and clear, not blurry.

In 1889, George Eastman, an American, invented film that was flexible enough to be rolled into coils. In 1891, American inventor Thomas A. Edison and his assistant William Dickson used this film to make 15-second movies.

Dickson punched holes along the edge of the film. Then he put the film into a camera called a Kinetograph that contained toothed wheels. These wheels pulled the film along at a steady pace. The films were shown in a machine called a Kinetoscope. A person watched the movie by dropping a coin into the machine and turning its handle to move the film forward.

Film tech

In 1895, two French brothers, Auguste and Louis Lumière, invented a camera that could film movies and also could be used to shine pictures on a screen. This projector worked by turning a crank. The crank turned toothed wheels that pulled the film past a light source behind a lens.

Now movies could be shown to many people at once instead of just one at a time. The Lumière brothers' first movies were simply scenes of people walking, parades, boats, and trains. People in the audience were so astonished, however, that they often leaped out of their seats in fright when trains thundered toward them on the screen!

At first, all movies were silent. A piano player or even an entire orchestra played music in the theater as the film rolled. The film also included panels of words to explain the story or provide dialogue.

The first movies with sound were shown in the 1920s and were called talkies. The first talkie was *The Jazz Singer,* released in 1927.

Early movies were all in black and white. Then, in 1932, a company named Technicolor® invented ways to shoot movies and print film in color. The first full-color film using the Technicolor® methods was a Walt Disney cartoon called *Flowers and Trees.* It was first shown on screens in 1932.

Today, filmmakers have all kinds of technology to work with to create exciting and entertaining movies for us. Computers add sound and music, create special effects,

and help directors edit the film. Editing involves cutting and rearranging filmed scenes to improve the telling of the story. Computers, in fact, have revolutionized filmmaking. The movie *Toy Story,* released in 1995, was the first full-length film to be made entirely with computers. *See also Camera; Television.* ●

NAIL POLISH

Nail polish has decorated fingers and toes for at least 3,500 years.

The ancient Chinese used a nail polish made of beeswax, egg whites, gelatin (from animal bones), and a thick tree sap. Color was added by mixing in dyes made from vegetables. Gold and silver polish was worn only by people of royal rank. Later, rulers switched to wearing red and black polish. Ordinary people had to settle for pale colors.

Most modern nail polish is a kind of paint called lacquer, similar to car paint. The lacquer is a mixture of many man-made, or synthetic, ingredients. People can choose from hundreds of colors as well as polishes with added fragrances or glitter. ●

And the Winner Is...

Every year, members of the Academy of Motion Picture Arts and Sciences vote to give awards to the best movies, actors, filmmakers, and other film artists and technicians (24 categories in all). The winners receive an Oscar, a 13.5-inch (35-cm) high, gold-covered statue of a knight holding a sword and standing on a reel of film. Three people claim they gave the statue its name. One of them, the Academy's librarian, said that the statue "reminds me of my Uncle Oscar."

What single person won the most Oscars? Walt Disney. He won 32. Two movies share the honor of winning the most Oscars (11 each): *Ben Hur* in 1959 and *Titanic* in 1997.

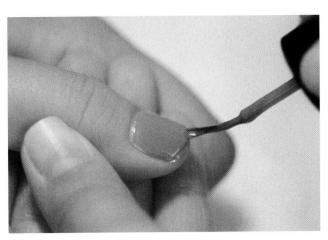

NEWSPAPER

A newspaper is a publication filled with stories about events, government, and business. It may also contain articles about such topics as sports, food, family, and pets as well as puzzles and comic strips. Some newspapers are published every day and are called dailies. Newspapers that are published once a week are called weeklies.

Many newspapers cover only local news. Others report national and international news, too. There are also newspapers that cover just one topic, such as the film industry or the stock market.

This city newsstand is loaded with newspapers from around the world.

Getting the news, then and now

In ancient times, people got the news from just one source. In Rome, people read the news by clustering around reports posted on walls in public squares. Two thousand years ago in China, reporters around the empire sent news back to the government. Eventually these reports evolved into an official newspaper for the ruling class.

People living in Europe in the 1600s could buy sheets of news called relations. The news, however, was old news by the time it was read. A daily newspaper did not appear until 1702. It was called *The Daily Courant* and was published in London.

American colonists first read an American newspaper in 1690. Only one issue was ever published, because the British government shut it down. But other newspapers later sprang up to take its place. One of these papers was the *Pennsylvania Gazette,* which Benjamin Franklin started in 1729. After America won its independence from England, newspapers flourished. By the mid-1800s, Americans had their choice of hundreds of newspapers.

Today, people can have newspapers delivered to their door or buy them at a newsstand. They can even read them on the Internet. *See also Comic Book; Paper.* ●

NUMBERS

Numbers are words and figures that describe amounts. The word *five*, for example, tells us how many fingers are on one hand. The word *twelve* indicates how many eggs are in a carton. Numbers are also symbolized by figures called numerals. The number three, for example, is represented by the numeral 3.

The ancient Egyptians used pictures as numerals. A simple line stood for the number one. Number ten looked like an arch. A pollywog stood for the number 100,000. People put numerals together and added them up to represent large numbers.

People in ancient Sumeria (now Iraq)

and India used a system that did not rely on adding numbers. Instead, the position of each symbol showed whether the numeral stood for a larger number or a smaller one. This kind of system spread to the Middle East about A.D. 600 and to Europe in the 1200s. It became known as the Arabic numeral system. The Arabic system included the numeral 0, which stands for zero.

$$5 + 5 = 10$$
$$5 - 5 = 0$$
$$5 \times 5 = 25$$
$$25 \div 5 = 5$$

Mathematical equations for addition, subtraction, multiplication, and division.

The Arabic system is the one we use today, though it is now called the decimal system. It consists of ten numerals ranging from 0 to 9. The position of a numeral in this system tells us whether it is a single unit, a "ten," a "hundred," and so on. *See also Alphabet; Calculator.* ●

OVEN

An oven is an enclosed space that cooks food by surrounding it with hot air. Modern ovens often have stovetops, too. A stovetop has open burners upon which pots and pans are placed and heated.

People have used ovens to cook since prehistoric times. Ancient Egyptians baked their bread 4,000 years ago in clay ovens fueled by wood. The ancient civilization of Sumeria (now Iraq) is credited with inventing the first stovetop oven. The first modern "kitchen range" was invented in England in 1780 by Thomas Robinson. It was made of cast iron and included an oven as well as a heating unit for boiling water. In 1802, an iron worker named George Bodley designed a range with an oven and a stovetop that looked much like modern ranges do.

Early ovens were messy and hard to clean. They burned coal or wood, which produced lots of soot. They also lacked temperature controls.

In the mid–1800s, the development of gas as a fuel led to the making of gas ovens. Later, electric ovens became available. In 1923, temperature-control devices for ovens were invented. Now cooks could control an oven's temperature with the flick of a knob. *See also Kitchen; Microwave Oven.* ●

Modern self-cleaning ovens heat up to 900°F (482°C) in order to burn grime off oven walls.

PAPER

Paper is made out of fibers that have been mashed together in water, pressed into a mat, and then dried to form sheets.

Today, most paper is made out of wood pulp. Wood pulp is wood that has been shredded and treated with chemicals. This process breaks down the stiff fibers in the wood and turns it into a soggy mass of fibers. Pulp used to make paper also includes wastepaper, old cardboard boxes, and wood chips left over from making lumber. The pulp is then cleaned and drained.

Next, the pulp may be bleached to make white paper. The pulp then goes into a machine that pummels, pounds, and squeezes it. This process makes the wood fibers bend more easily, which helps them pack together to form sheets. At this point, dyes may be added to produce colored paper. Other ingredients may also be added to produce papers designed for special purposes.

Finally, the pulp is spread out into sheets. The sheets are pressed by giant rollers to flatten and smooth them.

This symbol reminds people to recycle.

Papyrus and parchment

Five thousand years ago, the ancient Egyptians began using the papyrus plant to make thick sheets they could write on. They pounded the stems flat, dried them in the

Paper manufacturing is a major industry around the world. It involves many steps, from cutting down trees for pulp to shipping the finished paper. Giant machines process pulp and spread it into sheets or rolls.

sun, and cut them into sheets. Sheets of papyrus were rolled around a spool for storage and unrolled for reading. The word *paper* comes from the word *papyrus*.

Parchment was invented around 165 B.C. after the king of Egypt refused to send any more papyrus for the library in Pergamum (a city in what is now Turkey). Parchment is a very thin, smooth leather from animal skins that can be written upon.

The secret of paper

In the year A.D. 105, a Chinese man named Cai Lun is believed to have invented modern paper. He is said to have seen a patch of old rags and bits of tree bark floating in water. Cai Lun used a screen to scoop up the materials. When they dried, they formed a writing surface. In other versions of this story, Cai Lun is said to have been inspired by watching wasps chew wood to make their paper nests. Either way, Cai Lun began making paper out of rags, tree bark, old fishnets, and grassy plants.

Papermaking remained China's secret until the 600s. News of the process slowly trickled to other countries, but it did not

Recycled paper, like this one, made from used pieces of colored paper, newspaper, and cloth can be more interesting than the paper it is made with.

reach Europe until the 1150s. Native peoples of Mexico, however, seem to have discovered papermaking on their own around A.D. 400. They formed their sheets from the bark of fig trees.

From Rags to Paper

For centuries, rags were the main ingredient of paper in Europe and the United States. Paper manufacturers bought rags and even hired people to pick through garbage for rags. Pulp made from ground wood was not used until the mid-1800s.

Recycling paper

Huge amounts of paper are consumed today. Concern about cutting down forests to produce pulp has inspired many people to recycle paper.

Recycling paper involves cutting up boxes, newspapers, and other paper products to make pulp. Chemicals then remove the ink from the paper. Recycled paper is used to make new paper. *See also Book; Library.* ●

PEANUT BUTTER

Peanuts look like nuts, but they aren't. They are the seeds of the peanut plant and grow underground.

Peanuts are native to South America and have been harvested there for more than 3,000 years. In fact, Indians in ancient Peru made peanut butter! They ground the peanuts until they were mushy.

When Spanish and Portuguese explorers arrived in South America about 500 years ago, they tasted peanuts for the first time. After they returned to Europe, they introduced peanut farming there.

Peanut capital of the world

Peanuts also grew well in the southern part of the United States. But in the 1800s, only poor families and African slaves ate them. Some slaves called the peanut by its African name, *nguba*. Southerners pronounced this word as *goober*, which remains a slang term for peanut today.

The South was turned into the peanut-growing capital of the world almost single-handedly by a man who was born a slave in Missouri in 1861. His name was George Washington Carver. He grew up in freedom after the Civil War. As an adult, he developed crops that would help improve the soil by adding nutrients to

it. Peanuts were such a crop. Carver invented 300 ways to use products from the peanut plant so that people would grow it.

Surprisingly, though, credit for inventing modern peanut butter goes to another Missouri man—Dr. Ambrose Straub. In 1890, Straub developed a device that ground up peanuts into a paste. He introduced his sandwich spread at a fair in 1893. No one knows who teamed peanut butter with jelly. But after American soldiers in World War II had chowed down on peanut butter, its popularity soared.

How peanut butter is made

Peanuts that will be made into peanut butter first have their shells removed. Then they are roasted and their thin skins are peeled off. Finally, they are put into huge vats along with vegetable oil, salt, and sometimes sugar. There, they are ground up, stirred, and pumped into peanut butter jars.

Peanut plant

Today, half of America's peanut crop is used for peanut butter. About 720 peanuts are needed to make one pound (.45 kg) of peanut butter. ●

Pen

The pen was created when people needed a sharp tool to etch symbols on clay and wax tablets. These tablets were used about 6,000 years ago by the people of Sumeria (now Iraq). Later, the Egyptians made pens from the hollow stems of papyrus plants. They were dipped into ink, which flowed upward in the tube. The ink flowed out when the pen was pressed to paper made from papyrus plants.

Quills and nibs

Another type of pen that was used in olden times was made from the feather of a goose, swan, or duck. The tip of the feather was sharpened to a point and dipped into ink like the Egyptian pens. The feather pen was called a quill.

Metal pen points, called nibs, began replacing quills in the early 1800s. A factory in England started making steel nibs in 1828. Within 50 years, the quill was history.

Inventors of this time also began experimenting with pens that could store a large supply of ink. Such a pen, called a fountain pen, would let writers write without stopping to dip their pens into ink. Finally, in 1884, an American inventor came up with a fountain pen that worked well.

Fountain pens continued to rule until a Hungarian named Lazlo Biro designed a ballpoint pen in 1944. The ink of a ballpoint pen flowed easily onto paper and dried very quickly. In many European countries, ballpoints are still called "biros."

A ballpoint pen has a tiny ball, barely 1 millimeter (0.04 inch) in size. Ink flows down a tube inside the pen to cover the ball. The rolling ball applies the ink to paper in a steady stream. The ink in a ballpoint is so dense that the pen can draw a line the length of 20 football fields before running out. *See also Book; Paper; Pencil.* ●

The Link to Ink

Before the pen, there was ink. Ancient people made ink by mixing soot and colored dirt with animal fat. They used it to paint pictures with twig branches on cave walls. Early Egyptians made black ink by mixing soot with a gummy material from trees and drying it into cakes. Red ink was made with reddish iron ore. The writer wet the ink with water to use it.

PENCIL

A pencil is a writing device that contains a thin rod made of clay and graphite, called a lead. Graphite is a soft, dark form of the element carbon. Pencil makers mix graphite, clay, and water in different amounts to make leads that are soft or hard. Soft pencils, such as a #1 pencil, have more graphite and less clay than a hard pencil, such as a #3. After mixing, the leads are shaped and baked at about 1,900°F (1,038°C). Then they are enclosed in wooden holders.

Putting lead in the pencil

No one knows just who first thought of putting graphite into a holder to keep the user's hands clean. However, in 1565 a German-Swiss man, Konrad von Gesner, used a wooden holder filled with graphite to draw pictures and take notes.

Other early pencils consisted of bars of graphite wrapped in a cocoon of string. The user unwrapped the string as the graphite wore down. Some people put graphite into metal holders.

Erasers did not appear on pencils until 1858. No single eraser, however, seems to last as long as the pencil's lead. A modern pencil lasts long enough to write at least 45,000 words or a line 35 miles (56 km) long. *See also Eraser; Paper; Pen.* ●

PET

Pets are animals kept by people mainly as companions and playmates. They stand apart from animals raised for their milk, meat, hair, or hides, such as cattle, chicken, and sheep. Sometimes, however, people keep some of these other animals as pets, too.

The bond between humans and pets is a deep and ancient one, dating back to prehistoric times.

Most pets are domestic animals. A domestic animal is one whose long-ago ancestors were tamed and whose offspring were specially bred to produce tame, useful young animals. Very calm horses, for example, were bred with other gentle horses. Over thousands of years of careful breeding, people produced a horse that could be taught to pull a plow, allowed itself to be ridden, and even learned to round up other domesticated animals, such as cattle.

The first pets

People in almost all cultures throughout history have kept pets. Scientists believe that prehistoric people kept pets, too. These were likely to be baby animals that they found in the wild, such as wolf pups.

Scientists think that prehistoric people began domesticating wolves about 135,000 years ago. This idea is based on studies of modern dogs' genes. But clues in cave paintings and dog remains found where prehistoric people lived date back only 12,000 years. In any case, today's dogs, from the tiniest teacup poodle to the biggest St. Bernard, are descended from pet wolves kept by our ancestors.

Cats and other pets

Prehistoric humans also tamed goats, sheep, reindeer, and horses. Cats were probably domesticated at about the same time as the horse. The first pet cats were the kittens of African wildcats. The ancient Egyptians worshiped cats. Cat owners shaved their eyebrows off as a sign of sorrow when their cats died. The dead cats were often mummified and buried with great honor.

Other popular pets include birds, fish, hamsters, guinea pigs, and rabbits. Some people keep insects and reptiles as pets. ●

Pizza

Pizza is the most popular take-out food in the United States. In one day, Americans eat enough pizza to cover 100 acres of land. And that pizza is most likely dotted with pepperoni—America's favorite topping.

People did not slather tomato sauce on pizza until the 1500s. That's when Spanish explorers brought tomatoes back to Europe from South America, and Europeans started growing them.

Mozzarella cheese first appeared on pizza in 1889 when a pizza maker in Naples, Italy, wanted to make a special pizza in honor of a visit by Italy's queen. He made it red, green, and white, like the Italian flag. The result was a pizza covered with tomato sauce, basil sprigs, and cheese.

Pizza came to the United States with Italian immigrants in the late 1800s. Its popularity rose after American soldiers serving in World War II sampled it in Italy. *See also Spaghetti.* ●

Our Best Friend

After raising wolf pups they had rescued from the wild, prehistoric humans probably came to appreciate the wolves' skills as hunting partners and "guard dogs." At some point, they began breeding their tame wolves to produce loyal, useful companions. They may also have looked for such traits as superior smelling and tracking abilities, strength, size, and fur color. Over thousands of years of careful breeding, wolves evolved into the animals we call dogs.

Plastics

Plastics are materials that can be molded when they are heated and pressed. There are many different kinds of plastic. Soda bottles are made from a different kind of plastic than yogurt containers are. And these types of plastic are different from the flexible plastic fibers used to make nylon, vinyl, polyester, and other fabrics.

Most plastics today are made from by-products that result when petroleum, or oil, is processed. Some plastics are made out of coal, plants, or animal material. Plastic is useful not only because it can be molded, but also because it is light, yet strong and long-lasting.

Baseball helmet made of plastic.

What is plastic?

Plastic is made up of chains of very large particles called polymers. The element carbon is a main ingredient of these particles. Carbon bonds easily with many other elements to form new chemical compounds. That's why mixing chemicals together is one step in the process of inventing new plastics.

How plastic is shaped

Plastic is shaped into different products by using different methods. A plastic toy, for example, may be made by squirting melted plastic into a mold. A plastic mug may be formed by putting liquid plastic into two halves of a mold. The mold is then shut and heated until the plastic in both sides melts

All this plastic is ready for recycling. How to dispose of used plastic is a major environmental problem.

and sticks together. Still other products are made by putting a lump of soft plastic into a mold. Then air is blown into the plastic just the way air is blown into a balloon. This forces the plastic to take the shape of the mold, leaving an empty space inside. This is

Plastic objects come in all sizes, shapes, colors, and uses.

how plastic bottles are made. Plastic can also be heated and sprayed through a nozzle to make threads or squeezed in rollers to make plastic film and bags.

Recycling

One of the advantages of plastic is that it lasts a long time. This durability, however, creates a problem for our environment. Most discarded plastics do not decay, or break down, into small pieces that can be recycled naturally by the Earth. Instead, plastics accumulate in landfills and pollute the air with harmful gases when they are burned.

Researchers are working on ways to recycle more kinds of plastic and to find more uses for recycled plastic. They are also developing plastics that will break down into materials that will not harm the environment.

Meanwhile, we can all help protect our environment by recycling plastic bottles and other plastic items.

The first plastics

The first man-made, or synthetic, plastic was invented in the 1850s by the English chemist, Alexander Parkes. He called the plastic Parkesine. His plastic was not 100 percent synthetic. He used cellulose, a substance he obtained from plants. A few years later, John Wesley Hyatt, an American printer, bought the rights to Parkesine. He experimented with it, and turned it into a plastic he called Celluloid.

Celluloid quickly became very popular. It was used to make toys, jewelry, combs, and film. Celluloid, however, had a major disadvantage: it burned easily. It also cracked if kept in very cold conditions.

Plastics are everywhere

Then, in 1909, came Bakelite. Bakelite was the first plastic made using all synthetic materials. It was developed by the Belgian chemist Leo Baekeland. Bakelite products did not melt in heat. The new plastic was quickly used to make electrical parts, pot handles, countertops, telephones, and clocks.

Over the next century, many other kinds of plastics were invented. Today, plastic products are everywhere. Plastic toys entertain children. Plastic joints and limbs help some people walk. Plastic valves help some people's hearts beat. Plastic materials are found in buildings, cars, jets, boats, the space shuttle, and many other items. *See also Fabric.*●

PLAYING CARDS

A regular deck of playing cards consists of 52 cards divided into four suits, plus two jokers. The suits are called hearts, diamonds, clubs, and spades. The first two are red, and the latter two are black. Each suit contains 13 cards. Number cards include the cards from ace to 10. Picture cards are the king, queen, and jack.

Card playing is an ancient pastime. Over 1,000 years ago, people in China and India were playing card games. The Chinese used a variety of different card decks. One looked like paper money of the time. By the 1300s, cards had migrated to Europe, perhaps with traders, and were an instant hit.

Symbolic suits

In the late 1400s, the French designed the deck of cards with the four suits we still use today. Diamonds, which represent paving tiles found in markets, stood for traders. Hearts symbolized knights. The heads of weapons called pikes, or spades, stood for noblemen. Clovers, now called clubs, symbolized peasant farmers. The French also added queens to the deck.

Today there are hundreds of different card games, and each country has its favorites. In North America, popular card games include Blackjack, Gin Rummy, Crazy Eights, Old Maid, War, Go Fish, and Spit. *See also Board Game.* ●

POPCORN

Popcorn comes from a kind of corn plant. It produces kernels that pop when heated and puff up into light, fluffy treats.

Sweet corn, the kind of corn we nibble from the cob, is picked when its kernels are soft and moist. Corn for popping stays on the stalk until its kernels have become hard and dry. Deep inside each hard kernel, however, a bit of water remains.

Heating the kernels to a temperature of 400°F (204°C) boils the water inside and turns it to steam. The steam tries to escape, but the kernel's tough shell traps it. Pressure builds up inside each kernel until it

Corn used for popcorn is not picked until the kernels are hard and dry. Most of the world's popcorn is grown in Illinois, Indiana, and Nebraska.

explodes. Kernels that fail to pop are dried out inside or don't have enough water in them to cause the kernel to pop.

Exploding turns a popcorn kernel inside out. The fluffy white or yellow part of a piece of popcorn is the kernel's inner starchy part puffed up and facing outward. A piece of popcorn is up to 35 times bigger than the kernel it came from. That is why one cup of kernels can make about 30 cups of popcorn!

Really old popcorn

The native peoples of North and South America introduced European settlers to corn, including popcorn. According to legend, the Iroquois Indians brought a bag of popped corn to the Pilgrims' first Thanksgiving feast in 1621. The settlers liked popcorn so much, they began eating it in bowls with milk for breakfast.

Native Americans had discovered popcorn thousands of years earlier. Archaeologists found tiny ears of popcorn that are at least 7,000 years old in caves in Mexico. A bat cave in New Mexico held popped kernels of corn that date back 2,000 years, and a cave in Peru held 1,000-year-old popcorn. Some of these unpopped kernels still exploded when heated! ●

POTATO CHIP

Some say the potato chip was invented as a joke. Others say it was invented as an act of revenge. Either way, the potato chip's story starts in the early 1850s, at a restaurant in Saratoga Springs, New York.

The restaurant was quite fancy. One of the foods the customers liked best, however, were French fries. Today, we think of French fries as an inexpensive fast food. Back then, French fries were a new treat. They were thick slabs of fried potato, like the large fries we often call "steak fries" today.

One customer, however, thought the fries were too thick. He sent them back to the kitchen. The chef, George Crum, was directed to slice the potatoes thinner. In some versions of the story, Crum is annoyed by this order. In other versions, he decides to play a joke on the customer. But in all the stories, Crum does slice the potatoes extra thin and fries them in oil until they are toasted to a crisp.

The customer loved the crunchy potatoes, and potato chips became widely popular. By the 1920s, they were being sliced and fried in factories and sold in bags. Today, they are America's favorite snack food, with tortilla chips in second place.

It takes about four pounds (2 kg) of potatoes to make one pound (.45 kg) of potato chips. Water in the potato boils away as the thin slices fry. ●

QUILT

A quilt is a bedcover that consists of three layers: a layer of stuffing, or batting, that is sandwiched between a top and a backing. Stitching holds the layers together and stops the batting from moving around. The top of a quilt usually displays a colorful pattern.

Making and collecting quilts are popular hobbies today.

This method of sewing, called quilting, has also been used to make clothing throughout history. Quilted clothes were made centuries ago in China, India, the Middle East, and parts of Africa and Europe. They are still made and worn today.

Making quilts

Europeans brought quilting to North America, but in early colonial times, it was mostly well-off people who had quilts. For average folk, it was easier and cheaper to buy blankets. Quilting became more popular in the late 1700s when the invention of power looms made fabric more available.

Despite popular belief, most quilts were not made from scraps of leftover fabric. In fact, quilts were usually made from large pieces of fabric. Many women bought fabric just to use for quilting. Scraps left over from making clothing were often used for decorative purposes, but only because the seamstress chose to use them. Even patchwork quilts were usually made out of specially bought fabric.

Women who were very poor, however, did depend on scraps for making quilts. Making quilts was a way for these women to earn a little money. Even female slaves in the pre-Civil War South were able to earn money by making quilts.

Women usually worked on the quilt's top layer on their own. They would get together with other women to sew the top to the batting and backing. This part of the job had to be done with the cloth stretched tightly on a very big frame. Working together meant that quilts could be made quickly, and no one had to have a large quilt frame take up space in the house. These gatherings were called quilting bees.

Most early American quilts were made of cotton. Quilt makers especially liked calico cloth, a printed cotton fabric made in Calicut, India. The Amish people of Pennsylvania preferred to make wool quilts with bold patterns. *See also Fabric.* ●

RADIO

Radio waves are a kind of energy called electromagnetic radiation. They travel through the air in a pattern that looks like waves of the ocean, but you can't see them. The distance between the top of one radio wave and the top of the next one is called the *wavelength*. The number of waves that pass by in a second is called the *frequency*.

Another wave measure is called *amplitude*. This is the distance from the top of a wave to the bottom.

Changing the amplitude or the frequency of a radio wave allows it to carry sound. This discovery was the result of the work of many different scientists.

Before television, radios were the main home entertainment centers. They often came in large, fancy furniture pieces.

The first wireless

One of these scientists, Guglielmo Marconi, developed a way of sending telegraph messages by radio waves instead of over a telegraph wire in 1894. On December 11, 1901, Marconi sent a Morse code signal across the Atlantic Ocean from England to Canada. This was the first radio signal to cross the ocean. Thanks to Marconi's wireless, ships could now communicate across vast seas.

A Canadian inventor, Reginald Fessenden, made the first radio broadcast of voice and music on December 24, 1906. Fessenden figured out how to send radio waves in a constant stream rather than in small bursts like Morse code.

Radio stations

Each radio station sends out its signals at a specific frequency. When you select a station, you are tuning into the frequency at which that station is broadcasting. AM stations use one set of frequencies. FM stations use another.

How radios work

A radio receives radio waves via an antenna. The antenna turns these signals into electric pulses. Another device in the radio, called the tuner, sorts out the pulses depending on the station you have tuned the radio to receive. The tuner selects only those signals that match the frequency of the radio station you selected. Finally, a device called the amplifier pumps up the signals so that they are strong enough for you to hear. *See also Television.* ●

Radio Stations

The first radio stations went on the air in 1910, broadcasting both music and news. But regularly scheduled programs didn't start broadcasting until 1920. As the twentieth century unfolded, radio shows included soap operas, comedies, quiz shows, westerns, and adventure stories. Today, there are more than 27,000 radio stations around the world.

REFRIGERATOR

Since ancient times, people have used the power of ice and snow to keep food from spoiling. Over 3,000 years ago, the Chinese chilled food cellars with ice and snow from mountaintops and frozen lakes.

Ice-cold storage

People in England in the 1700s stored ice from lakes in underground icehouses. They packed the ice in salt and fabric to keep it cold. Americans packed ice tightly in sawdust and stored it in cellars or wooden sheds.

In the late 1800s, people began storing food in iceboxes. At the top of the icebox, separate from the food, there was room for a chunk of ice. The ice absorbed heat and melted. As it melted, it cooled the air around it. Cool air is heavier than warm air, so the cool air moved down to where the food was stored. There the cool air absorbed heat and rose back up, where it melted the ice some more and cooled down again.

A better icebox

A refrigerator is an improved version of the icebox. Instead of ice, it uses a liquid called a refrigerant. A device called a compressor pushes the refrigerant into two sets of coils. In the evaporator coils, the liquid refrigerant becomes a gas and takes out heat from the inside of the refrigerator. In the condensor

THEN AND NOW. *Old-fashioned iceboxes (left) dripped water and were messy. Ice also had to be purchased regularly from icemen. Modern refrigerators (above) are energy efficient and easy to clean. Many also make ice cubes and dispense cold water.*

coils, the gas becomes a liquid again and takes more heat out of the refrigerator.

The first refrigerator was invented in 1834 by Jacob Perkins, an American. Its compressor had to be cranked by hand. Compressors posed problems for the first electric refrigerators, too. They were run by motors so large and loud they were kept in the basement or a nearby room away from the refrigerator! In 1927, the General Electric company produced a quieter fridge with its compressor on the top. In 1934, the compressor was moved to the bottom, where it still is today. *See also Frozen Food; Kitchen.* ●

RESTAURANT

In ancient China, city streets were lined with shops where cooks dished up steaming bowls of noodles. In ancient Rome, people bought cheese, bread, and other foods at the marble counters of "snack bars." Street vendors in other cities sold food, too. Roadside inns provided food for travelers.

Other places to eat were taverns and cafes. Taverns served hearty, inexpensive food as well as alcoholic drinks. Cafes, which sprang up in France in the late 1600s, served tea, coffee, and desserts.

A new kind of eating place was started in 1765 in France by Monsieur Boulanger, who opened the first "restaurant." The name he chose let customers know that they would be "restored," or refreshed, by the food served there. Boulanger sold soups, cooked meats, and other prepared foods, which people ate inside the restaurant at private tables.

New and improved restaurants

During the next 100 years, restaurants continued to grow in popularity and in numbers. One chef, Georges-Auguste Escoffier, improved restaurant cooking and service by organizing cooks and kitchen workers. Each was assigned particular tasks, such as slicing vegetables or baking pastries. This eliminated much extra work. Escoffier's ideas are still at work in modern restaurants. He also wrote a cookbook containing nearly 3,000 recipes.

In the 1900s, Americans enjoyed an ever-widening choice of restaurants. The dining cars of trains offered fabulous food. Casual restaurants called diners served hearty meals at low prices. In the 1950s, it was popular to eat at drive-in restaurants, where food was served to people while they sat in their cars in the parking lot.

Fast food

In 1955, a salesman named Ray Kroc started a chain of hamburger restaurants called McDonald's®. The chain specialized in selling the same kind of food at each restaurant. The food was also prepared and served quickly. Other fast-food restaurants began appearing on the scene. Today, McDonald's® and other American fast-food restaurants are popular around the world. *See also Hamburger; Pizza.* ●

Eating out at restaurants is a treat for friends and family alike.

ROAD

A road is a route designed to let people and their vehicles or beasts of burden travel easily from one place to another. It can be as simple as a country lane or as complex as a six-lane highway.

Early humans had little need of roads. They simply followed the paths made by wild animals. Once human communities began trading goods and services, they needed roads that were wide and strong enough to support the heavy traffic of humans, camels, horses, donkeys, and others.

As far back as 800 B.C., the ancient Chinese were building roads. Sometimes, the builders deliberately put bends in the road to trip up the speedy flight of the evil spirits they believed existed. The Inca people of South America built over 15,500 miles of road by the year 1520—a system that included a 2,250-mile coastal highway.

The champion road-builders of ancient times, however, were the Romans. Their impressive highway system paved the way for future road-builders. Roman engineers built straight roads by leveling soil, then topping it with a layer of sand. Into this roadbed, they set large, flat stones called "flagstones." Next, they spread a layer of concrete followed by a hard surface of lava rock.

Gentle curves for water

Most important, the Romans shaped the roads so that they curved gently down from the middle to the sides. This curving, called cambering, allows water to drain into ditches along the sides of the road. The Romans built more than 50,000 miles (80,000 km) of roads that stretched from northern England to Africa. To compare, a highway from New York to San Francisco measures about 3,000 miles (4,828 km).

Modern road-builders study the soil and water-drainage patterns before starting to build. Heavy machines clear the way and level and compact the soil. The road itself is a sandwich of materials. First, a layer of crushed rocks and gravel covers the hard-packed soil. Heavy machines compress these materials before they are covered with macadam, which is a mixture of hot tar or asphalt and stones. Like Roman roads, modern roads are cambered. *See also Car.* ●

ROLLER SKATES

Most kids who skate today ride on in-line skates—skates with wheels lined up in a row. Long before in-line skates existed, though, people used roller skates—what today's "bladers" call "quads."

Roller skates have four wheels arranged in two pairs. One pair is attached at the front of the skate, the other at the heel. At first, skates rolled on wooden or metal wheels. Now wheels are made of polyurethane—a hard, shock-absorbing plastic that grips pavement and gives a smoother ride than either wood or metal.

The very first roller skates had only two wheels per skate. They were invented about 1760 by Joseph Merlin, a maker of musical instruments in Belgium. In 1863, American James Plimpton improved skate design by using four wheels per skate.

In-line skates

Today, roller skates have been largely replaced by in-line skates. The basic in-line skate is a padded boot with four wheels that are lined up in a straight row from toe to heel, surrounded by a plastic or metal frame, called a chassis. A heel brake is located on the right skate. Children's skates have only three wheels, because the boots are smaller. Racing skates have five wheels.

Blades

Two brothers named Scott and Brennan Olson are credited with inventing in-line skates in 1980—for ice hockey players. Both brothers liked ice hockey—a sport that can be played outdoors only in winter, when ponds and lakes are frozen. In warm weather, players head indoors to ice rinks. Using in-line skates, hockey players can skate across pavement as if they were skimming across ice. Such skates are very useful for training in the off-season.

Hockey players quickly adopted the skates, and many others soon did the same. By the mid-1980s, the Olsons' business, now called Rollerblade, Inc., took off. In-line skaters used the brand name Rollerblade® to create a new sports jargon. Although many brands of in-line skates are now available, skaters still often refer to in-line skating as "blading" and skates as "blades." *See also Hockey; Ice Skates.* ●

SALT AND PEPPER

Salt and pepper are seasonings added to food to make it tastier. Salt is a mineral, called sodium chloride, found in rocks and in the ocean. Pepper is a spice made from the fruit of a climbing vine.

Salt was the first seasoning used to flavor people's food. Archaeologists have found salt mines in Europe that date back 8,500 years. These scientists think that humans began salting food after they stopped being full-time hunters and started growing most of their food.

Plants contain very little salt, if any. But humans need salt to live. Without salt, cells cannot work properly. So humans needed to salt their food to replace the salt they had been getting from a diet rich in meat. They also used salt to preserve food.

Salt and pepper are the most popular flavor enhancers of all time.

Salt money

Salt played an important role in world trade in ancient times. People fought wars to gain control of salt supplies. Nations grew rich by trading salt to other nations. Roman soldiers even received a portion of salt along with their wages. This "salt pay" was called a *salarium,* from *sal,* the Latin word for "salt." Later, this word became *salary,* which is still used to describe a person's pay.

Today, we get salt by pumping water into salt mines. The salty water is pumped out, and the salt is removed from it. We also get salt by collecting ocean water and letting the sun dry it up, leaving salt behind.

Pepper power

Pepper has also been highly valued. The ancient Greeks prized it as a medicine. In ancient Rome, flavoring one's food with pepper was a sign of high rank. In Europe during the Middle Ages, a pound of pepper could be traded for a pound of gold.

The pepper vine first grew only in the East Indies, an area that now includes Indonesia and parts of India and Southeast Asia. Today, the vine is also grown in Brazil and the African island of Madagascar.

The vines' fruit is a little round berry called a peppercorn. Black pepper is made by grinding dried, green, unripe peppercorns. White pepper is made by removing the dark outer skin of dried, red, ripe peppercorns, then grinding them into powder. ●

SANDWICH

The sandwich gets its name from an Englishman, John Montagu, the fourth Earl of Sandwich. Montagu lived from 1718 to 1792. He loved playing cards and often skipped meals so that he could keep on playing his favorite games.

In 1762, Montagu played cards in London for 24 hours straight. During this marathon, he told his servant to bring him slices of cold beef between pieces of bread. The earl was able to eat this food without stopping his game—and without getting his cards greasy. The meal soon became widely known as a sandwich. *See also Bread.* ●

This super-size sandwich is known by many names: hero, submarine, hoagie, grinder, and poor boy.

SATELLITE DISH

Today it is common to see satellite dishes attached to houses and apartment buildings. These dishes pick up TV signals broadcast by communications satellites orbiting the Earth at a height of about 22,223 miles (35,786 km). Cable TV companies and television stations also receive TV signals from such satellites.

A communications satellite zips along at about 7,000 miles (11,300 km) per hour in order to keep up with the Earth's rotation. If you could see it from the ground, the satellite would look as if it were standing still. Such a satellite is called a geostationary satellite, which means it is always above the same spot on the Earth.

A home satellite dish must be positioned so that it points directly at the satellite. Because the satellite stays over one spot on Earth as it orbits, the satellite dish doesn't need to move around to keep track of it.

How the dish works

The curved shape of the dish gathers the signals beamed from the satellite and aims them at the antenna that sticks out from the dish. Devices in the dish strengthen the signals and turn them into electric signals, which are sent to the television set. There, the signals are converted into a television picture with sound. *See also Television.* ●

Many people are subscribing to satellite TV companies for their TV service. To stop people from using the service for free, TV signals are "scrambled" so that only subscribers with the proper devices can watch shows.

SCHOOL

In ancient times, only boys were educated in schools. Girls stayed home and learned to sew and cook, although some also learned to read.

Greek, Roman, and Egyptian boys learned to read, write, and do math as well as ride horses and wrestle. In ancient China any boy could attend school if he were smart and worked hard and his family could pay the small fee.

In the Middle Ages, upper-class European boys and girls were often educated by being sent to live with relatives and work for them. Some boys worked in castles, where they might be assistants, or squires, to knights. Some studied in monasteries. The children of peasants worked on farms. Children who weren't peasants or nobles often went to work as apprentices to learn a trade.

The first American schools

In the early 1600s, religious leaders urged that all children learn to read so they could study the Bible. Village schools soon appeared in Europe. In colonial America,

THEN AND NOW. *Early classrooms in America had only a few basic teaching aids. Many of today's classrooms are comfortable, high-tech learning centers equipped with computers.*

most children were schooled at home, where they also did household and farm work. Then, in 1647, a Massachusetts law dictated that every town with 50 families or more had to offer a school where children could learn to read, write, and do math. If the town had 100 families or more, the school had to teach Latin and Greek and prepare students for college, too. Families were not required to send their children to school, but schools had to exist. A small fee was charged to attend.

One-room schools

An early American schoolhouse was often a one-room log cabin heated by a fireplace.

Parents supplied the firewood, and the children cut it to size. Children whose parents did not provide wood willingly were made to sit in the room's coldest corners. Windows were made of oiled paper, not glass. There were no chalkboards. Children sat on benches at desks made of boards. Girls might attend school in summer while the boys were schooled the rest of the year.

The colonial school day began as early as 7 A.M. and lasted until 5 P.M., with two hours for lunch. Children attended classes six days a week. Most girls and many boys quit school after the age of eight.

Free public schools

In the late 1700s, log-cabin schools began to be replaced by buildings made of wooden boards, painted red. Girls attended schools more regularly. It was even suggested that they would benefit from higher education.

Students at this time wrote assignments on little chalkboards called "slates." They also wrote with lumps of coal, or with quill pens using homemade ink. Teachers expected their students to work hard and were very strict. Troublemakers were put in the corner wearing cone-shaped "dunce caps" or whipped with a stick or strap.

In 1827, Massachusetts once again led the way, this time by founding the first free, state school system paid for by taxes. In 1848, a school in Quincy, Massachusetts, began a nationwide trend by grouping children by age into grades and teaching them in separate classrooms. Gone was the one-room schoolhouse.

Modern classrooms

By the mid-1800s, many northern states had high schools as well as elementary schools. Free public schools became the rule in the South in the late 1800s. After 1850, schooling became compulsory for all children between the ages of 6 and 14.

In the early 1900s, most schools were big, brick buildings filled with classrooms, with a playground outside. The classrooms had chalkboards, and each child had his or her own desk. Over time, specialized rooms were added, such as science laboratories, gyms, libraries, and art and music rooms.

Today, many children attend preschool before entering kindergarten or first grade. Elementary schools generally end after fifth grade. Middle schools run from grades six through eight. High schools start with ninth grade (also called freshman year) and end after twelfth grade, or senior year. *See also Book; Library; Paper; Pen.* ●

Early Learning

Young students in colonial America learned the alphabet with the help of a hornbook. This was a wooden paddle with a covering made of thin, see-through horn. Beneath this protective covering was a piece of paper printed with letters and some prayers. Strips of birch bark were sometimes used instead of paper. After the children learned their ABCs, they moved on to readers, or primers.

Scissors

The scissors we use to cut thread, paper, and other items are made up of two sharp blades that are linked to each other by a screw. The blades have loops in their ends so that the user can insert his or her fingers. Scissors of this type are called pivot scissors. Scissors longer than six inches in length are called shears.

Spring scissors

The first scissors did not have screws. They consisted of two blades connected at one end by a curved piece of metal. The curved metal worked like a spring. The blades were pushed together to make a cut, then sprang back open to get ready for the next cut.

These early scissors existed nearly 5,500 years ago. They were invented after people learned how to work with metals. This event marked the end of the Stone Age and the beginning of a period called the Bronze Age. Bronze, a mixture of copper and tin, was the first metal used to make scissors.

People used these early scissors to cut hair, plants, and animal skins. Spring scissors were used throughout much of the ancient world. About 1,000 years ago, wealthy Europeans used spring scissors made of gold and silver studded with pearls and diamonds. Workers, such as tailors, used scissors made of bronze, brass, or iron.

Even though pivot scissors were invented 2,000 years ago, spring scissors remained in common use up until the 1500s. Spring scissors were simply less expensive, because they were easier to make. Pivot scissors became popular after 1761 when Robert Hinchcliffe, an English metalworker, found a way to make strong scissors quickly and cheaply. He used a kind of steel that produced very strong blades.

Today's scissors are made of different kinds of steel and are made in different shapes, depending on their use. There are blunt scissors for children's use, and sharp scissors for cutting fabric or paper. People who sew use jagged pinking shears to cut fabric so its ends don't fray. Surgeons use stainless-steel scissors while operating. ●

One-Handed Shears

Over the centuries, people have invented scissors in many shapes and sizes to suite different purposes. Metalworkers of 500 years ago, for example, used very big shears that were designed to be used with one hand. One of the blade's handles had a sharp point that could be rammed into a large chunk of wood. This held the shears still so that the metalworker could easily use it just by pressing on the other handle with one hand. The other hand remained free to hold the metal that needed to be cut.

SILVERWARE

Silverware, or cutlery, is the variety of knives, forks, and spoons used at the table for serving and eating meals.

The knife is the oldest of the three. It has existed for at least 35,000 years. Early knives were made of stone and bone. They were used for cutting up the bodies of animals killed for food. About 5,500 years ago, people learned how to work with metal and began making sharp metal knives.

It was common up until the late 1600s for Europeans to use knives for spearing food at the table and carrying it to their mouths. These sharp knives were also used as weapons. In the Middles Ages, it was fashionable to eat with two knives.

Blunt knives

Then, in 1669, King Louis XIV of France made pointed knives illegal. All knives were to have blunt, rounded ends so that people could not stab each other, either at the table or in the street. Today's table knives have blunt ends, too, except for special sharp knives used for cutting steak and other foods.

The spoon is the second-oldest piece of silverware. Archaeologists have found stone-age spoons made out of shells, wood, animal horns and bone, and clay. The ancient Egyptians used bronze spoons, while rich Greeks and Romans dined with silver spoons.

The fork probably began as a two-pronged, or forked, stick used for spearing cooked food in Stone Age campfires. A forked stick does a better job of gripping a piece of meat than a stick with just one point. The ancient Greeks and Romans used metal forks with two prongs for cooking and for holding meat still while carving it.

Forks were not used for eating at the table, however. Kings and nobles in the Middle East used serving forks at least 1,400 years ago. Forks did not appear in Europe until 1100, when they were brought to Italy by traders.

Individual forks

Another 600 years went by before table forks began appearing regularly on tables in Europe. Forks did not arrive in England until the 1600s. Even then, most people thought forks were a silly tool and laughed at those who used them.

During all this time, the fork's design kept changing. Forks with two prongs, or tines, did not hold food well because the long, straight tines stood far apart from each other. Food fell off between them. Adding a third tine made the fork a better eating tool. In the 1700s, a fourth tine was added. The tines were also curved slightly so that food could be scooped up as well as speared. *See also Dishes.* ●

SKATEBOARD

The first skateboards were called scooters. They were made by children who nailed four-wheeled skates to boards and then rolled down hills and along sidewalks on their homemade toys. Kids have made scooters in this way for about 70 years.

Store-owner Bill Richards turned the scooter into a skateboard in 1959. He and his son bought skate parts from a roller-skate manufacturer and attached them to boards. The skateboards went on sale in his California surf shop.

Sidewalk surfers

The wooden skateboards became popular with surfers grounded by calm seas, as well as with kids who did not surf. As skateboarding caught on, skateboard design changed. Plastic boards were sold as well as wooden ones. New wheel axles were invented in 1963 that helped skaters lean into turns.

The skateboard fad faded for a few years. Then, in 1973, another Californian, Frank Nasworthy, used a new kind of wheel for skateboards. It was made out of a plastic called polyurethane. Polyurethane wheels made skateboarding faster and smoother. They did not skid the way metal wheels did on tight turns. The new wheels made all kinds of stunts possible, and skateboarding enjoyed a new burst of popularity.

A good-quality skateboard is usually made of layers of maple wood glued together. It is slightly curved in front and back. The polyurethane wheels come in different sizes to suit different kinds of skating maneuvers. They are attached to special axles called trucks. The trucks swivel so that the skater can move and turn the board just by leaning from side to side. *See also Roller Skates.* ●

SNEAKERS

Advances in making rubber led to the invention of the sneaker. In the 1830s, American inventor Charles Goodyear came up with a way to make rubber that would not harden and crack in cold weather or melt in hot weather. This rubber found its way into shoe making by the 1860s.

People in England liked the rubber-soled shoes with canvas tops. The rubber soles gripped the ground, making them useful for playing games outdoors.

James Greenwood, an American writer, called the shoes *sneakers* because they allowed a person to walk quietly and sneak up on someone.

New materials and designs

High-topped sneakers for children called Keds® were sold in 1917. Basketball sneakers came on the market a year later. By the late 1900s, sneakers had evolved into tennis shoes, running shoes, and walking shoes.

Sneaker design kept changing as

sneakers grew in popularity. In 1950, manufacturers added little metal-rimmed holes to the sides of sneakers to help sneaker-clad feet get fresh air. Shoes with nylon tops instead of canvas ones came on the market in 1967. In the 1970s, Bill Bowerman, a track coach, experimented with designing a new sneaker sole that would help runners dash without slipping. In a moment of inspiration, he poured rubber on a waffle iron and created the waffle sole now found on many running shoes.

New materials and designs continue to change the look and feel of sneakers. Today, nearly half the number of shoes bought in the United States are sneakers. ●

SOAP

Bars of soap are made by combining a fat, such as animal fat or vegetable oil, with a chemical compound called an alkali. Soap's cleaning power comes from the structure of its molecules. Each molecule is like a magnet with two strong poles. One pole is attracted to particles of dirt, grime, and grease. It attaches itself to these particles, pulls them away from the object being cleaned, and holds them in the water. The other pole is attracted to water. As it pulls the water, it drags the dirt along and out with the rinse water.

A short history of clean

The Phoenicians, who lived in what is now Lebanon in the Middle East, made soap out of goat fat and ashes 2,600 years ago. Greeks, Romans, and other Europeans took the idea and began making soap, too.

By the 1100s, some cities in Europe had become soap-making centers. People also made soap at home. Up until the Civil War, many people in the United States saved fats from cooking to make soap. Soap made in factories that people purchased from stores began replacing homemade bars in the late 1800s.

Unfortunately, soap is not good at cleaning everything. In fact, it sometimes causes bathtub rings, streaks on clothing, white build-up on glasses, and dull hair. As a result, scientists developed different types of cleaners, such as detergents and shampoos. *See also Bathtub.* ●

Soccer

Soccer is perhaps the world's most popular sport. It is certainly the most popular in Europe and South America.

Soccer is played by two teams consisting of 11 players each. Each team tries to get the ball into the goal of the opposing team. The goalie is the only player on the field who can touch the ball with his or her hands. Other players may only kick the ball or butt it with their heads.

The soccer ball is made of leather or rubber and weighs about one pound. A professional soccer game lasts 90 minutes, divided into two halves.

Soccer has its roots in many ancient games that involved two teams vying for control of a ball. In the Middle Ages, villages in England played soccer-like games against each other. These games got so rough that in 1314 King Edward II banned them.

By the end of the twentieth century, soccer became a very popular sport among American girls and boys.

Rules for soccer were officially established in 1863 by the London Football Association. (Outside the United States, *soccer* is called "football.") In 1885, professional soccer teams started up in England. The game also traveled overseas wherever British sailors and traders went.

Every four years, two soccer teams vie for the sport's international grand prize, the World Cup. The World Cup began in 1930 and has been held every four years since then. *See also Football.* ●

Soda

Soda, pop, and soda pop are all names for a popular soft drink made with water, syrup, and bubbles of the gas carbon dioxide. The syrup is basically a mixture of flavors, sweeteners, and dyes. The bubbling water is called carbonated, or soda, water.

Good-health drinks

In the past, drinks made from soda water were thought to be aids to good health. The idea that plain soda water is good for a person's health dates back to the time of ancient Rome. The ancients, however, simply bathed in the water. Later, people began drinking it.

The first bubbly soft drinks sold in bottles were made by Jacob Schweppe in 1783 in England. Schweppe's soda waters were sold in drugstores because they were believed to have healthful medical effects. By the 1800s, soda water mixed with fruit-flavored syrup had become popular. In the

mid-1800s, an Irish doctor invented a new drink—ginger ale.

Soda was considered to be a health tonic in the United States, too. Soda was bought and consumed at drugstore "soda fountains." Many pharmacists invented their own custom-blended syrups. The syrups became sodas when the counter worker added soda (carbonated) water to them. Sodas were made up for each customer.

Some of today's well-known sodas trace their roots to syrups first brewed as medicines. In 1886, pharmacist John S. Pemberton in Atlanta, Georgia, stirred up a caramel-colored syrup for people with stomach ailments. It was later mixed with carbonated water. This drink became Coca-Cola. Other sodas have similar histories. Pepsi-Cola was invented by pharmacist Caleb Bradham in 1898. Dr Pepper was first served in Waco, Texas, at the Old Corner Drug Store in 1885. •

SPAGHETTI

In Italian, *spaghetti* means "little strings." These strings of pasta are made by pressing dough through little holes in a metal disk. The dough is made of water and a wheat flour called semolina. Spaghetti comes in different thicknesses, ranging from extra-thin strands to twirly, thick ones.

In the 1700s and 1800s, travelers to Italy claimed that people ate spaghetti by scooping it up with the hand, tilting back the head, and dropping it in. The recommended method today is simply to twirl a few long pieces around a fork.

Sun-dried spaghetti

Spaghetti was made by hand in the past. Today, complicated machines turn out pasta in dozens of shapes, both curly and straight. The first spaghetti factory was set up in Naples, Italy, in 1800. Its spaghetti strands were hung up to dry in the sun. Perhaps this practice is how the myth that spaghetti grows on trees got started.

Spaghetti has been served with many different kinds of sauces over the centuries. Tomato sauce, however, did not cover spaghetti until the 1500s. Tomatoes were unknown in Europe until explorers brought them back from South America.

Likewise, spaghetti and meatballs did not team up until Italian immigrants arrived in the United States and invented the dish there. *See also Pizza.* •

STUFFED ANIMAL

Children have played with animal toys for thousands of years. Archaeologists have found animal toys dating back 4,000 years in ancient India, Egypt, and other lands. The animals range from little cats with movable tails to horses pulling wagons.

Two companies that became famous for making stuffed animals, Steiff and Gund, were both started in the late 1800s. And they are still making stuffed toys today.

Steiff animals were born in Germany, in the home of a seamstress named Margarete Steiff. She began sewing felt elephants in 1880 and selling them by mail. Soon she was also sewing bears, donkeys, and dogs. The Steiff company started making teddy-type bears and other animals with movable limbs in 1902. Two years later, Steiff animals became popular in the United States.

Teddy bears

By chance, teddy bears were born in the United States in 1902, the same year the Steiff teddy bears were born in Germany. Teddy bears are named after President Theodore "Teddy" Roosevelt. Roosevelt liked to hunt. However, he refused to shoot a young bear that was being held captive for him to kill. A cartoon appeared in newspapers about Roosevelt and the bear, which gave a Brooklyn, New York candy-shop owner and his wife the idea of making stuffed bears. They called the toys Teddy bears and put them in the store window. The bears were an instant hit. Teddy bears are still beloved today. *See also Doll.* ●

SUPERMARKET

A supermarket is a giant grocery store. People walk through a supermarket's aisles, pick out what they want, and buy it. This method of food shopping was unheard of less than a century ago.

In the past, people shopped at a variety of small stores for different foods. They visited a bakery for bread, a butcher shop for meat, a grocer for vegetables, or stopped at different stalls in a marketplace. In a small, corner grocery store, a clerk behind the counter fetched goods for the customer.

Then, in 1916, a store called Piggly Wiggly opened in Memphis, Tennessee. It was the first grocery store where customers selected their own goods. Customers walked through a turnstile to enter the store. They had to walk down every aisle in the store, as in a maze, to reach the cashier. After paying the bill, they exited through another turnstile.

The first supermarket opened in 1930 in Jamaica, New York. It was called King Kullen and was named after its owner and designer, Michael Cullen. The store offered only about 300 items, but the prices were low. Soon others copied the idea, and new supermarket chains sprang up.

Modern supermarkets have bakeries and delis and offer many other kinds of cooked foods, uncooked foods, and non-food items. Some supermarkets include coffee shops, video rentals, and small banks.

Today, some people bypass stores altogether. They buy their groceries over the telephone or the Internet and have them delivered. ●

Today's supermarkets sell an amazing number of food and non-food products.

TAPE

Tape used for sticking things together is made of cellophane, fabric, paper, or other material that is coated on one side with a light glue, or adhesive.

The tape we use today developed from masking tape, invented in 1925. The American inventor, Richard Drew, was a researcher for the Minnesota Mining and Manufacturing Company (now called 3M).

At that time, many cars were painted in two colors. This meant that one color had to be covered up while the other was painted on. Workers applied homemade glue to paper and stuck it onto the part of the car body to be protected. Often, the glue pulled off the paint when the paper was removed.

Sticky solutions

Drew created masking tape, a fabric tape about two inches wide with adhesive along its back that did not pull off the paint. This success inspired Drew to invent another kind of tape in 1930. He put adhesive on the back of cellophane, a new material invented in 1924. But the tape, called Scotch™ Tape was not a success until the tape dispenser was invented in 1935.

In 1961, 3M designed Scotch™ Magic Transparent Tape. This tape did not yellow with age as the first tape did. It could also be written on. Tape that could be removed and reapplied became available in the 1980s. ●

TELEPHONE

"Mr. Watson! Come here! I want you!" These were the first words spoken in the world's first telephone conversation on March 10, 1876. The speaker was Alexander Graham Bell. The listener was his assistant, Thomas Watson. After years of work, Bell and Watson had invented the telephone.

Bell was a professor of speech. He also worked with deaf people and had devised a method for teaching them to speak. On the side, Bell experimented with ways to transmit sound because he wished to make a device that would help deaf children talk. Watson was an electrical engineer. With his skills, he was able to turn Bell's ideas into working devices.

In 1877, Bell started the Bell Telephone Company. A year later, telephone switchboards were already humming. Workers connected callers and receivers by plugging and unplugging wires.

The telephone went through many design changes after its invention. Thomas Edison, for example, came up with a new kind of earpiece and mouthpiece for phones that transmitted sound more clearly. He is also credited with making "Hello" a standard phone greeting.

Today's phone lines relay speech as well as text and images sent by fax machines. They also link up computers worldwide via the Internet. Mobile or cellular phones are linked by radio transmitters instead of wires. *See also Computer; E-mail; Internet; Radio.* ●

Transmitting sounds

It had been known for many years that sound traveled by vibrating the air. Electricity, too, had been investigated by many scientists. In 1844, people sent the first long-distance messages over a metal wire with a new invention, the telegraph. A telegraph carried messages in the form of coded electrical impulses.

Bell's invention, however, used electrical impulses to send actual sounds. His telephone contained a metal sheet, or membrane, that vibrated and turned sounds into electrical signals. Vibrating membranes in the telephone receiver then turned the signals back into sounds.

THEN AND NOW. *Early phone systems required operators at huge switchboards (below) to connect calls. Today's cell phones (left) are wireless and can connect you directly to someone on the other side of the world.*

TELEVISION

A television set turns electrical signals into pictures on the set's screen. The incoming signals cause devices called electron guns to shoot streams of tiny particles called electrons at the back of the TV screen. The back of the screen is coated with a substance called phosphor, which glows when it is hit by an electron.

In a color set, electrons from three separate guns cause different dots in the phosphor to glow in different colors. In a black-and-white TV, all the dots of phosphor glow white. Either way, the glowing dots blend together in the viewer's mind's eye to form one picture.

The birth of TV

Much of the credit for inventing TV usually goes to an American inventor born in Russia, Vladimir Zworykin. In 1923, he designed a TV camera that could broadcast pictures and a picture tube that could receive those pictures.

The first television picture was broadcast on October 2, 1925, by a British inventor, John Logie Baird. He beamed an image of a puppet's head onto a screen.

Regular TV broadcasts began in England

THEN AND NOW. *Early TV sets (above) had small, round screens and fancy cabinets. Today's sleeker TV provides sharper, clearer pictures.*

in 1936 and in 1939 in the United States. It was not until the late 1940s that Americans began buying TV sets in great numbers. At first, there were only black-and-white models. Color TV became available in 1954, but sets were expensive. In 1972 color sets outnumbered black-and-white ones in the United States for the first time.

Cable and satellite

TV sets receive signals in several ways. They can pick up broadcast signals with an antenna, like the earliest TVs did. They can also receive signals via cables. Cable TV systems first started in the 1950s to bring TV to people in places where hills or tall buildings interfered with broadcast signals. Today, some people choose to use a satellite system, in which a satellite dish picks up signals and routes them to the TV.

In the late 1990s, a new development called high-definition television (HDTV) became available. HDTV provides pictures that are sharper, brighter, and wider than the ones seen on regular television. Like the first TV sets of the late 1940s, HDTV sets are very expensive, and HDTV broadcasting is still limited. *See also Movie; Satellite Dish.* ●

THERMOMETER

A thermometer is a device that measures temperature. A mercury thermometer consists of a thin glass tube that contains mercury and is marked with lines of measurements. Mercury is silver-colored; alcohol mixed with red dye is often added to make the thermometer easier to read.

At high temperatures, the mercury climbs up the tube. At low temperatures, it drops down. The level of the mercury matches up with a line of measurement, and this is the temperature reading. Mercury thermometers are usually placed under the tongue to take a person's temperature.

Mercury Thermometer

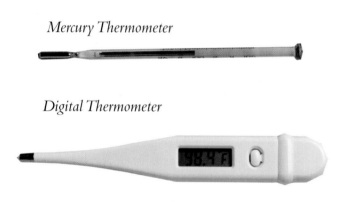

Digital Thermometer

Non-mercury thermometers

A liquid crystal display (LCD) thermometer contains tiny particles that change color in response to very small temperature changes. An LCD thermometer may simply be placed on the forehead to take a person's temperature.

A digital thermometer reads temperatures electronically. Some use a flexible metal probe to read the temperature, then display the result in numbers almost instantly. One type of digital thermometer is placed in the ear, where it measures the temperature of the eardrum.

Most human temperature thermometers use the Fahrenheit scale of measurement, developed by Gabriel Daniel Fahrenheit in 1720. On this scale, ice melts at 32°F, water boils at 212°F, and a person's normal body temperature is 98.6°F. On the Celsius scale, invented in 1742, 0°C is the melting point of ice, 100°C is the boiling point of water, and 37°C is normal body temperature. ●

TOILET

Flush toilets connected to a sewer system have only been around for a little over 100 years. Since ancient times, people have struggled with the problem of how to get rid of human waste.

Some ancient cities built waste systems that worked like ours do today. A brick sewer system dating back nearly 4,000 years was dug up in Pakistan. The great palace at Knossos, on the island of Crete near Greece, had a toilet for the use of the queen. Water flowing through clay pipes beneath the toilet carried away waste.

Large cities in the ancient Roman Empire also had underground sewer systems consisting of ditches through which water flowed. Toilets in public restrooms were stone seats with holes over these ditches.

People living in cities without sewer systems used toilets that worked rather like cats' litter boxes. Wealthy people in ancient Egypt, for example, might have a toilet in the house that consisted of a seat placed over a container of sand. Slaves or servants were responsible for cleaning the container.

Sewer systems in most cities fell into disrepair during the break-up of the Roman Empire in 476 A.D. In Europe, sanitary habits practically vanished. People used small receptacles called chamber pots and tossed the waste out the window into the street. They also used public latrines that were placed right over waterways.

Castles in medieval Europe had toilet rooms that contained a stone or wooden seat. Drains in the castle carried waste out of the castle and into the moat or a special cesspit. The cesspit was cleaned at night.

The first flush toilets

An early flush toilet was invented in 1449. It was designed by an Englishman named Thomas Brightfield. This toilet was flushed by water kept in a tank above it. Flush toilets did not catch on at first because they smelled badly. They allowed odors from the cesspits to enter the house.

Americans also relied on chamber pots and outdoor latrines called outhouses or privies. Waste went into a pit or a bucket. Children often had the task of discarding waste collected in a bucket.

Then, in 1775, an English watchmaker named Alexander Cummings invented a flush toilet that had a curved pipe in its base instead of a straight one. The S-shaped pipe trapped a pocket of water in its bend. This

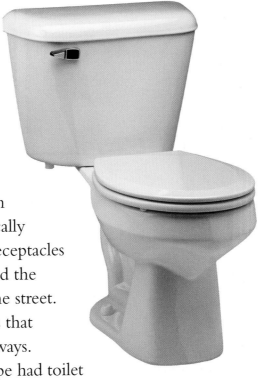

THEN AND NOW.
Flush toilets old (right) and new (above) operate on the same basic principle. Water from the tank is released into the bowl and with the help of gravity flushes waste away. Modern toilets do the job more quickly, cleanly, quietly, and with less water than older toilets.

stopped smells from coming back up the pipe and into the house. Cummings called it a "stink trap." Modern toilets still rely on curved pipes to block odors.

In 1872, an English plumber named Thomas Crapper improved the way the toilet tank worked. He is often credited with inventing the toilet, which is untrue.

Modern toilets use less water than old ones. These low-flow toilets use about 1.6 gallons (6.0 liters) of water per flush compared to the 3 or 4 gallons (11 or 15 liters) used by old toilets. ●

Toothbrush and Toothpaste

The first toothbrushes were simply sticks shredded at one end, called chew sticks. The ancient Egyptians used them 5,000 years ago. Arabic people did, too, and people in parts of Africa still do today.

Toothbrushes with bristles were first used in China about 1,000 years ago. The handles were made of wood or bone. The bristles came from hogs.

A better bristle brush

Hog-bristle toothbrushes were brought to England about 350 years ago. The brushes never became popular because people disliked the bristles' stiffness. They preferred soft horsehair brushes instead. These brushes did a poor job of cleaning, however. They also harbored moisture and germs.

Toothbrushes entered the modern age when nylon was invented in the 1930s. Nylon bristles were stiff, strong, and dried quickly so that they did not provide a home for germs. The first nylon brushes were very hard and hurt people's gums, so researchers worked to design a softer nylon, which debuted in the 1950s. Electric toothbrushes came on the market in 1961.

Toothpaste has also been used for thousands of years. The ancient Egyptians made toothpaste out of powdered stone and vinegar. The ancient Greeks used burnt eggshells. Crushed coral, chalk, salt, baking soda, and powdered limestone have all served as toothpastes, too.

A modern tube of toothpaste contains many ingredients. One you might see is calcium carbonate—the same material that forms chalk and limestone. This finely powdered material is called an abrasive. It is rough enough to scrub teeth clean without harming their outer surface, or enamel. Another important ingredient is fluoride. Fluoride is a chemical that strengthens enamel and helps prevent cavities. Fluoride added to drinking water has the same effect.

Toothpaste may also have carrageenan, which is made from seaweed and keeps the ingredients from separating. Other ingredients include preservatives, coloring, thickeners, flavors such as mint, and soap to make the toothpaste frothy when brushing. *See also Comb and Hairbrush.*●

Trading cards

Trading cards are cards that are swapped, bought, sold, collected, displayed, and played with. Both adults and children use trading cards.

The most famous kind of trading card is the baseball card. Baseball cards feature photographs of baseball players and statistics

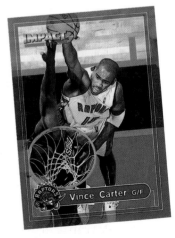

This trading card features the Toronto Raptors guard/forward Vince Carter.

about their playing. The first baseball cards were put in cigarette packages in the 1880s. This type of baseball card died out 40 years later, only to come to life again in 1933 when baseball cards were put in packets of bubble gum. It was mostly kids who collected these cards. "Flipping" cards was a good way to win new cards—or lose the ones you had.

This trading card features Yankee shortstop Derek Jeter, voted Most Valuable Player in the 2000 All-Star Game.

Trading cards also feature football, soccer, and basketball stars. There are also non-sports cards devoted to movies and TV shows, such as *Star Trek, Star Wars,* and *Pokémon.* Other trading cards have featured everything from rock stars and model trains to mathematicians. *See also Comic Book.* ●

Traffic light

A traffic light directs traffic by telling drivers when to stop, go, and turn. A standard traffic light features a red light at the top, an amber light in the middle, and a green light at the bottom. Many lights also feature red, yellow, and green arrows.

A traffic light may hang above the street or be mounted on a pole along the street. Both kinds of lights are attached to control boxes that are run by timers.

Many traffic lights are programmed to change automatically. Some can be reprogrammed by a computer. Others respond to sensors that can detect waiting cars. The sensor is often an electric wire that stretches underneath the road and then goes up to the light. The wire sets up a magnetic field. When a car stops above the wire, the magnetic field sends a signal to the traffic light.

A short history of traffic lights

The first traffic light was invented by J.P. Knight, a British engineer who worked on railway signals. It was set up in a London street. Red meant "stop" and green meant "caution." This first traffic light, however, was powered by gas, and it exploded.

Early traffic lights were mostly hand-operated. They were placed in towers at intersections and a worker changed the signals.

In 1918, the familiar red-amber-green trio appeared in New York City's hand-operated light towers. Such towers gave way to electric traffic lights, invented in 1923 by an American named Garrett Morgan. Automatic lights first directed traffic in 1926 in London, England. *See also Car; Light Bulb.* ●

TRAIN

A train is a string of cars pulled or pushed along a track by a locomotive, which is an engine on wheels. The track consists of two parallel steel rails attached to crossbeams, called ties. A bed of gravel lies beneath the track. A train wheel is designed to ride along rails. It has a rim around its edge that hangs over the rail. This kind of wheel is called a flanged wheel and keeps the train from slipping off the track.

The first trains rolled in the mid–1500s in Europe. They were small coal-mining cars that rode on wooden beams and were pulled by humans or horses. In the late 1700s and early 1800s, horses also pulled wagons along rails on city streets in parts of Europe.

In the 1700s, engineers discovered ways of putting steam to work in engines that powered machines. The first steam locomotive began chugging in 1804. It was designed by an English engineer named Richard Trevithick. His locomotive was strong enough to pull wagons loaded with tons of iron. Unfortunately, the engine was so heavy, the rails often snapped beneath it.

Steam trains carrying freight and passengers began crisscrossing England in 1830. Railroads started up in the United States in 1830, too. On May 10, 1869, the

THEN AND NOW. *Early American steam locomotives (right) were famous for their pointed "cowcatchers" up front, big headlights, and smokestacks spewing clouds of smoke and steam. The first underground trains, or subways, were also steam-powered. Today's high-speed trains run on electricity.*

East and West Coasts were finally linked by rail when the last section of track of the Transcontinental Railroad was nailed down in Promontory Point, Utah. Cities and towns sprang up along the nation's railways.

The caboose, the last car of a freight train in which trainmen rode, was often red or yellow. Its job is done today by electronic equipment.

To make steam, a locomotive burns coal inside an oven. The fire heats up air, which causes water in a tank to boil. The boiling water then turns into steam. The power of the steam forces the wheels to move. Excess steam billows out of the smokestack in white clouds; the dark clouds are the smoke from the fire in the oven.

Steam engines were mighty machines. These "iron horses" weighed as much as 280 tons (254,000 kg) when fully loaded with water and coal. Steam engines built after 1925 could pull 100 freight cars.

Diesel and electric trains

Another kind of engine, however, would eventually replace the steam engine. This was the diesel engine, which runs on heavy fuel oil. A diesel engine is an "internal-combustion engine," like an automobile engine. It was invented by Rudolf Diesel, a German engineer. A diesel engine is more efficient than a steam engine, which means it converts more of the energy in its fuel into motion than a steam engine does.

The first trains with diesel engines went to work in the 1940s. They replaced steam engines entirely during the 1950s.

Electric locomotives, which were invented in the 1870s, became more widely used, too. Electric locomotives get their power either from an electrified "third rail" on the ground or from an electric power line hanging over the track. Because electric engines do not produce fumes or smoke, they were especially useful for underground trains, called subways. The first subway, however, was powered by steam. It was introduced in England in 1863.

Trains continue to carry freight and passengers worldwide today. The world's fastest train is the TGV, a French electric train that can zoom up to 200 miles (320 km) per hour. *See also Car; Wheel.* ●

One-Track Trains

A monorail is a train that rides on a track with only one rail. Its rubber wheels reduce friction, making the ride quieter and faster than in traditional trains. A maglev train also runs on a single track, but it doesn't touch it. The train floats on a magnetic field created by magnets embedded in the track and the train itself. The magnetic force hurls the train forward. In the future, maglevs may speed up to 300 miles (480 km) per hour.

UMBRELLA

The first umbrellas protected people from sunshine, not rain. They were carried by people living in the hot, dry lands of ancient Egypt and Mesopotamia (what is now Iraq). These umbrellas were made of feathers, leaves from palm trees, and papyrus, which was an early form of paper.

In ancient times, umbrellas symbolized power and importance. In some cultures, only members of the royal family could stand beneath umbrellas, which were held by servants. In ancient China, servants shaded the nobility with umbrellas covered with gold and jewels. Chiefs in Africa also stood beneath umbrellas borne by servants.

Rain protection

It was also the fashion for ancient Greek and Roman noblewomen to carry dainty umbrellas, called parasols. Roman women sometimes oiled their paper parasols to make them waterproof. People in China started doing the same thing about 1,500 years ago.

Europeans did not begin using umbrellas until about 500 years ago. Even then, they were carried only by priests, as a symbol of importance. Then women began carrying them, too. Feathery, lacy parasols became popular in France in the 1700s. Men did not carry umbrellas until the late 1700s.

Most umbrellas in those days were heavy, clumsy devices made of oiled cotton and bone ribs. They often leaked. In 1829, special silk made in France replaced cotton. Eleven years later, an English inventor designed steel ribs. The umbrella finally became a useful guard against the rain.

Today, umbrellas come in many colors, patterns, and sizes. They range from tiny fold-up models to giant beach umbrellas. ●

VELCRO®

Velcro® is the trade name of a popular fastener that consists of two pieces of nylon fabric. One piece is covered with hundreds of tiny hooks. The other piece is covered with hundreds of little loops. When the two pieces are pressed together, they stick to each other because the hooks snag the loops.

The idea for Velcro® came from the prickly burrs of seedpods.

Velcro® was the brainstorm of a Swiss man named George de Mestral. He got the idea for a new kind of fastener while hiking in Switzerland in 1948. During the hike, bristly seedpods from plants clung to his clothes and to his dog's fur. He examined the pods under a microscope and saw that they were covered with little hooks.

This gave de Mestral the clever idea of trying to make his own version of the seedpod's design. He succeeded in creating a "locking tape" in the early 1950s after working with a textile weaver in France. De Mestral called the locking tape *Velcro®*, a word formed from two French words. *Vel* comes from *velour,* which means "velvet," and *cro* from *crochet,* which means "hook."

Velcro® was first used to fasten shut astronauts' space suits and help their boots stick to spacecraft floors. Over the next few decades, the hook-and-loop fastener found its way onto ski clothing, toddlers' shoes, wallets, book bags, watchbands, toys, and medical equipment. *See also Tape.* ●

Vending machine

A vending machine is a device that takes in money and returns a product in exchange.

The first vending machines were called "honesty" or "honor" boxes. They appeared in England in the 1700s and dispensed tobacco products. An honor box was operated by putting in a coin, then opening the lid. People were trusted to be honest and take just what they paid for, in the same way that people are expected to take just one newspaper from a modern newspaper vending machine.

In 1883, vending machines that sold postcards appeared in subway stations in London, England. In 1888, vending machines arrived in the United States. They sold chewing gum and other candies. In 1902, a restaurant called Horn & Hardart's Automat opened in New York City. To buy food at the Automat, people put coins into slots, then turned knobs to open little glass doors and take out plates of food. Vending machines in the United States began selling cigarettes in 1926 and sodas in 1937.

Soup to nuts…and then some

In the decades that followed, vending machines were installed in factories and offices. They offered coffee, soup, and packaged foods as well as candy and soda. By the late 1900s, vending machines seemed to be everywhere, from schools and stores to hospitals and airports. The new vending machines dispensed far more than candy. They have sold items ranging from stamps and film to frozen beef, dried squid, tiny toys, eggs, live fish bait, gasoline, pizza, and even blue jeans! ●

VITAMINS

Vitamins are substances that living things need in order to grow, function properly, and stay healthy. They work by taking part in different chemical reactions in the body. Most vitamins come from eating nutritious foods. The body does not produce most vitamins. The only vitamins human bodies make are vitamin D (essential for bones and teeth) and vitamin B_{12} (needed for red blood cells). The body can make vitamin D from sunlight. Bacteria living inside our intestines produce vitamin B_{12}.

The discovery of vitamins

Long before people knew about vitamins, they knew that eating certain foods cured or prevented certain illnesses. They did not know why or how this happened, but they knew that they needed to eat a variety of foods in order to stay healthy.

A lack of vitamin C, for example, causes a disease called scurvy. Sailors in olden times often fell sick with this disease and could die while on long voyages. Sometimes, a captain would lose half of his crew to scurvy.

Eating citrus fruits, such as lemons and limes, and certain vegetables, such as cabbage, prevented scurvy. Dutch sailors in the 1500s knew this, but British sailors didn't adopt this habit until the late 1700s.

In 1906, F. Gowland Hopkins, an English scientist, discovered that animals needed certain ingredients in their diets in order to thrive. These mystery ingredients were given the name vitamins in 1911. The name, which emphasizes how "vital" vitamins are for life, was invented by a Polish-American scientist named Casimir Funk.

In 1912, Funk discovered the first vitamin, a chemical compound that was named vitamin B_1, also known as thiamine. A lack of thiamine causes a disease called beri-beri, which is marked by loss of weight and paralysis.

Vitamins for health

Over the past century, scientists have discovered other vitamins and how they work. This research has led the U. S. government to suggest the amount of each vitamin a person should have each day. The amounts are known as the Recommended Daily Allowance, or RDA.

New scientific discoveries sometimes spur the government to require that certain vitamins be added to commonly eaten foods. One such vitamin is folic acid, a B vitamin. Folic acid is essential for healthy red blood cells and prevents certain birth defects in babies. Folic acid is now being added to bread and other grain products.

A person who eats a varied and balanced diet can get all the vitamins he or she needs from foods. Many people choose to supplement their diet with vitamin tablets. Taking large doses of vitamins can be harmful. ●

WASHING MACHINE

Today's washing machines soak and scrub clothes at the push of a button. The clean clothes are then tossed into a dryer or attached to a clothesline with pegs to dry in the sunshine. Washing clothes wasn't always this simple, though.

In the past, washing clothes was back-breaking work. Women carried clothes to a stream or river. There they pounded the clothes against flat rocks in the water. The wet clothes were then squeezed dry and draped over bushes to dry.

Early inventions

The job got a little easier in the late 1700s with the invention of the scrub board. This was a wooden frame that held a ridged wooden or metal surface. It was placed in a tub full of soapy water. Clothes were rubbed up and down the ridges to remove the dirt.

Still, washing clothes was hard, exhausting work. Two hundred years ago, American women often set aside Monday to do the laundry—or at least start the job, which could take much of the week.

In 1847, the clothes wringer was invented. This device consisted of horizontal rollers attached to a crank. Wet clothes were fed into the rollers, which squeezed out much of the water. This made drying clothes a little easier.

The first washer

The first washing machine appeared in Europe in the 1800s. It was simply a tub attached to a crank. Turning the crank made the tub shake. The shaking stirred up, or "agitated," the water, soap, and clothes inside the tub. The crank had to be turned for many hours.

In the United States, an Indiana man named Bill Blackstone invented a washer in

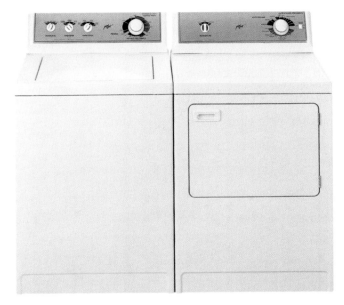

Today's washing machines (left) and dryers (right) offer a wide range of settings for different types of fabrics.

1874 that worked in a similar way. It became a hit. Soon, other inventors designed washers that were powered by gas or steam.

Electric washers began cleaning clothes in 1911, but they were still just tubs filled with water and attached to wringers. Over the next 30 years, however, engineers came up with many improvements.

One improvement was an "agitator" with blades. The blades shoved the clothes in the water, pushing out the dirt. Another innovation was the spin-dry washer, which had a metal basket with holes inside its tub. The tub and basket whirled around, forcing water out of the clothes. Spin-dry washers replaced wringer-washers in the 1950s. ●

Wheel

The wheel is one of the most important things that humans have ever invented. Wheels gave people in ancient times the ability to move heavy loads over long distances. Using wheeled vehicles, people could travel farther and trade with other people who lived great distances away. Today, wheels still power vehicles and are also hard at work inside machines in the form of gears.

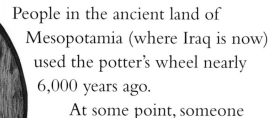

A copy of a Sumerian wheel

Inventing the wheel

Before the wheel's invention, people could only drag loads themselves or use animals to drag them. This was hard work because it was difficult to overcome the friction that stopped the load from moving easily along the ground. Friction is a force that acts against motion. It is caused when surfaces rub against each other.

No one is quite sure just how the wheel was invented. Many scientists think the potter's wheel was the first wheel. A potter's wheel lies on its side. The potter places a lump of clay on the wheel and then makes it spin. As the wheel spins, the potter forms the clay into a round pot or bowl of clay with his or her hands.

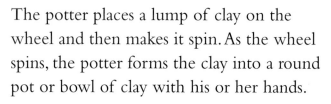

Stone wheel

People in the ancient land of Mesopotamia (where Iraq is now) used the potter's wheel nearly 6,000 years ago.

At some point, someone thought of turning the wheel upright so that it rolled along the ground. Perhaps this person connected the potter's wheel with a method people had long used to move heavy objects. This method involved laying out a row of logs and pushing an object across them. The logs rolled the object along much like a conveyor belt moves suitcases at airports today.

Archaeologists have found clues that point to Sumeria (located in southern Mesopotamia) as the birthplace of wheeled vehicles in about 3500 B.C. Tombs in this region contain wheeled carts, chariots, and wagons dating back 5,000 years.

Spoked wheels

The first wheel was made of three slabs of wood held together by bands of wood. This kind of wheel is called a tripartite, or three-part, wheel. It rolled around a wooden axle in the middle of the wheel.

People in other lands were quick to adopt the Sumerians' invention. By 2000 B.C., wheeled carts and wagons were a common sight throughout the Middle East, Europe, and Asia. Some wheels had metal rims to protect the wood from wearing down. Others were studded all around with copper nails. People in China and Turkey used stone wheels when wood was not available.

The big wooden spoked wheels on these wagons in Death Valley, California, are typical of the wheels that helped American pioneers cross the country.

A new kind of wheel, however, also began rolling on roads: the spoked wheel. People had begun to cut sections out of the center of tripartite wheels to make a wheel that was lighter and moved more easily. Eventually, the cut-out wood was replaced with strong struts, or spokes, of wood.

Spoked wheels were particularly useful on chariots, which needed to be fast, light, and easy-to-drive for use in battles and in races. The spoked wheel, which could be made larger and lighter than the tripartite wheel, enabled charioteers to drive quickly, even on rough ground.

Over the centuries, people improved on the wheel as they made new discoveries. They lined axles with leather and oiled them with animal fat or vegetable oil so that they turned more easily, just as we grease car axles today. Sometime around A.D. 1500,

wheels called "dished wheels" were invented. The spokes on these wheels were angled to make wheel rims wider for carrying wide loads on narrow roads.

New wheels for new uses

Steam engines began turning wheels in the mid-1700s. About 50 years later, paddle wheels moved steamboats and steam locomotives began puffing. Trains used a new kind of wheel called the "artillery wheel," which could support heavy vehicles. These wheels were made of strong cast iron and had wedge-shaped spokes.

In the 1870s, light wheels with wire spokes were invented for bicycles. The first cars had wooden-spoked wheels. By the 1930s, cars were rolling on steel wheels.

The invention of tires helped speed up traffic. Tires reduced friction and allowed wheels to move faster. Air-filled rubber tubes called pneumatic tires came into use in the 1880s. Modern car tires, which do not contain rubber tubes, were invented in 1948. *See also Car; Bicycle; Train.* ●

Working Wheels

Over time, people found other ways to use wheels in addition to moving vehicles. They developed waterwheels, which carried water from lower to higher areas. Wheels called millstones turned to grind grain. Spinning wheels spun wool into yarn. Clock wheels helped keep more accurate time. Ferris wheels provided fun and thrills at amusement parks.

Yo-yo

A yo-yo is a toy made of two discs attached by a post, which rolls up and down on a string. Chinese people bounced ivory yo-yos on silk strings 3,000 years ago. The ancient Greeks played with yo-yos 2,500 years ago.

French people discovered the yo-yo in the 1700s, covered it with jewels, and called it *l'emigrette*. Next, the yo-yo skipped over to England, where it was dubbed a "quiz." Yo-yos finally bobbed up and down in the United States in the 1860s. People called the toy a "bandalore." The name "yo-yo" comes from a word used to describe the toy in the Philippines, where it became very popular in the early 1900s.

In the late 1920s, the yo-yo caught the eye of an American salesman named Donald Duncan. He began making and marketing the toy, which soon became wildly popular. Yo-yo fads swept the nation again in the 1950s and 1960s. In 1962 alone, over 25 million yo-yos were sold. Yo-yos enjoyed a burst of popularity again in the late 1990s. ●

Zipper

A zipper is a fastener made of two rows of tiny teeth that lock together when a slide rolls across them. The zipper got its start as a device called a "clasp locker and unlocker for shoes." It was invented in 1893 by an American named Whitcomb Judson, as a way for people to open and shut their high-top shoes in one quick and easy motion.

The clasp locker consisted of two rows of hooks and eyes, which were pulled together by a sliding device. It was a good idea, but Judson's device often got stuck or popped open.

A zipper with teeth

In 1913, a Swedish-American named Gideon Sundback who worked for Judson turned his boss's device into a success. He designed a fastener that was almost exactly like the modern zipper, equipped with teeth instead of hooks. Soon the fastener was zipping shut gloves, pouches, boots, money belts, and Navy men's flying suits.

In 1923, a company that made rain boots added Sundback's fasteners to their product. The boot was called the Zipper Boot. Since then, Sundback's fasteners have been called *zippers. See also Velcro®*. ●

BIBLIOGRAPHY

BOOKS

100 Inventions That Shaped World History by Bill Yenne (San Francisco: Bluewood Books, 1993)

A Kid's Guide to the Smithsonian (Washington, D.C.: Smithsonian Institution Press, 1996)

Book by Karen Brookfield (New York: Alfred A. Knopf, 1993)

Car by Richard Sutton (New York: Alfred A. Knopf, 1990)

Costume by L. Rowland-Warne (New York: Alfred A. Knopf, 1992)

Cotton by Millicent E. Selsam (New York: William Morrow and Co., 1982)

Cyberspace and the World Wide Web by David Jefferis (New York: Crabtree Publications, 1999)

Eyeglasses by Margaret J. Goldstein (Minneapolis: Carolrhoda Books, 1997)

Film by Richard Platt (New York: Alfred A. Knopf, 1992)

Fire! by Joy Masoff (New York: Scholastic, Inc., 1998)

From Wax to Crayon by Michael Forman (Chicago: Children's Press, 1997)

How Is a Crayon Made? by Oz Charles (New York: Simon and Schuster Books for Young Readers, 1988)

Invention by Lionel Bender (New York: Alfred A. Knopf, 1991)

Machines in the Home by Rebecca Weaver (New York: Oxford University Press, 1992)

Mistakes That Worked by Charlotte Foltz Jones (New York: Doubleday, 1991)

Money by Joe Cribb (New York: Alfred A. Knopf, 1990)

Money by Robert Young (Minneapolis: Carolrhoda Books, 1998)

Sleep On It! by Kevin Kelly and Erin Jaeb (Chicago: Children's Press, 1995)

Sports by Tim Hammond (New York: Alfred A. Knopf, 1988)

Steven Caney's Invention Book by Steven Caney (New York: Workman Publishing Co., 1985)

The History of Making Books (New York: Scholastic Voyages of Discovery, 1996)

The Kids' Book of Chocolate by Richard Ammon (New York: Atheneum, 1987)

The New Way Things Work by David Macaulay (Boston: Houghton Mifflin, 1998)

The Origins of Everyday Things (Pleasantville, NY: The Reader's Digest Association, 1999)

The Sun Was the First Clock and Other Facts About Time by Helen Taylor and Stephen Sweet (Brookfield, CT: Copper Beech Books, 1999)

Toilets, Toasters, and Telephones by Susan Goldman Rubin (San Diego: Harcourt, Brace & Co., 1998)

Vanilla, Chocolate, and Strawberry by Bonnie Busenberg (Minneapolis: Lerner Publications, 1994)

Wheels! The Kids' Bike Book by Megan Stine (Boston: Little, Brown, 1990)

Why Doesn't My Floppy Disk Flop? and Other Kids' Computer Questions Answered by the Compududes by Peter Cook and Scott Manning (New York: John Wiley, 1999)

(Continued on the next page)

Bibliography (Continued from previous page)

CD-ROMS

Encarta

Grolier Multimedia Encyclopedia

World Book Multimedia Encyclopedia

The New Way Things Work by David Macaulay

WEBSITES

www.brainpop.com/tech/

Animated cartoons answer your questions about how such machines as microwave ovens and CD players work. Fun quizzes test your knowledge and amaze you with interesting facts.

www.enchantedlearning.com/inventors

You can find information about inventors and inventions by clicking on any alphabet letter, century, or category (such as food, fun, transportation). Many entries show a picture of the inventor or the invention.

www.howstuffworks.com

Text, illustrations, and animations reveal how various machines function.

www.pbs.org/wgbh/aso/tryit/tech/#

Colorful timelines and information about the history of household appliances and other items.

PHOTO CREDITS

INDEX

supermarket, 100–101

synthetics, 9, 45, 52

Syria

    alphabet, 6

    board game, 16

    glass, 50

T

tape, 101

Teddy bear, 100

telephone, 102

television, 91, 103

    commercials, 33

thermometer, 104

tires, 115

toilet, 104–105

toothbrush, 106

toothpaste, 106

trading cards, 106–107

traffic light, 107

train, 108–109

Transcontinental Railroad, 109

transistor, 37

transportation

    airplane, 58

    balloon, hot-air, 9

    bicycle, 15

    car, 26–27

    jet plane, 58

    space shuttle, 27

    train, 108–109

    wheel, 114–115

Turkey

    library, 62

    mail, 64

    wheel, 114

U

umbrella, 110

URL (Uniform Resource Locator), 57

V

vacuum tubes, 36

Valentine's Day, 52

Velcro®, 110

vending machine, 111

vitamins, 112

volts, 14

W

washing machine, 113

Washington, George, 7, 55

watches, 30–31

watt, 63

wavelength, 85

wheel, 114–115

windows, 50

wool, 44

World Series, 11

World Wide Web, 57

wristwatches, 31

X

X rays, 66

Y

yo-yo, 116

Z

ZIP (Zoning Improvement Plan), 64

zipper, 116